BANK STREET COLLEGE OF EDUCATION

THE BEST CHILDREN'S BOOKS OF THE YEAR

2008 EDITION

Books Published in 2007

SELECTED BY THE

CHILDREN'S BOOK COMMITTEE

ABOUT THIS LIST

THE CHILDREN'S BOOK COMMITTEE AT BANK STREET COLLEGE OF EDUCATION strives to guide librarians, educators and parents to the best books for children published each year. The current nonprofit committee that reviews the books includes educators, librarians, authors, parents and psychologists who share a passion for the world of children's literature. Young reviewers from all over the country, ages 2-18, read and evaluate many of our books as well.

In choosing the annual list, reviewers consider literary quality and excellence of presentation as well as the potential emotional impact of the books on young readers. Other criteria include credibility of characterization and plot, authenticity of time and place, age suitability, positive treatment of ethnic and religious differences, and the absence of stereotypes. Nonfiction titles are evaluated for accuracy and clarity. Each book accepted for the list is read and reviewed by at least two committee members and then discussed by the committee as a whole. In addition, the committee gives awards in the areas of fiction, poetry and nonfiction.

This year's centerfold is

NEW BEGINNINGS: LIFE IN A NEW LAND

Starting a new life in a new location has challenged and inspired people throughout history. It is especially pertinent in today's world. We have listed books which reflect the struggle and euphoria of moving from place to place.

The Committee has listed several excellent books on its website which are more appropriate for older readers. The list, available without charge, may be found at
www.bankstreet.edu/bookcom/teen.html

THIS YEAR'S AWARDS

The 2008 Josette Frank Award
for
Home of the Brave
by KATHERINE APPLEGATE
published by Feiwel and Friends

This award is given each year to honor a book or books of outstanding literary merit in which children or young people deal in a positive and realistic way with difficulties in their world and grow emotionally and morally. The prize to the author of the award books has been generously provided by The Florence L. Miller Memorial Fund.

The 2008 Claudia Lewis Award
for
Here's a Little Poem:
A Very First Book of Poetry
collected by JANE YOLEN and ANDREW FUSEK PETERS,
illustrated by POLLY DUNBAR
published by Candlewick Press

and

This Is Just to Say:
Poems of Apology and Forgiveness
by JOYCE SIDMAN, illustrated by PAMELA ZAGARENSKI
published by Houghton Mifflin Company

This award is given for the best poetry book or books of the year for young readers.

The 2008 Flora Stieglitz Straus Award
for
Ballerina Dreams
by LAUREN THOMPSON, photos by JAMES ESTRIN
published by Feiwel and Friends

and

Who Was First? Discovering the Americas
by RUSSELL FREEDMAN
published by Clarion Books

This award is given for a nonfiction book that serves as an inspiration to young readers.

Awards from 1943-2007
http://www.bankstreet.edu/bookcom/past_winners.html

THE CHILDREN'S BOOK COMMITTEE

Illustrations by

The Young Reviewers and the Teen Reviewers work with the Committee under the direction of Todd Jackson and Alex Grannis. The 14 to 18-year-olds evaluate some of the books for the "Teen List" which you can find on our website: **www.bankstreet.edu/bookcom/teen.html**

CONTENTS

TIPS FOR PARENTS

- Share your enjoyment of books with your child.

- Talk over your reading.

- Continue to read aloud to your child even after he or she reads independently.

- Encourage your child to choose a book to read aloud to someone else.

- Broaden your child's horizons by helping to select from a wide range of subjects.

- Encourage your child to read whatever he or she enjoys even if it appears to you to be too easy or too hard.

- Let your child see your enjoyment of your own reading.

- Find time for your child to visit and browse in libraries and bookstores.

KEY

★	Outstanding merit
	Babies & Toddlers
B	Board Book
NE	New Edition
E	Easy to read
M	Mature reading
·	SERIES TITLE (series books follow)
(4-6)	Age range
P	Paperback
	Graphic novel

UNDER FIVE

Macky Pamintuan 2007

ABeCedarios: Mexican Folk Art ABCs in English and Spanish
by Cynthia Weill, and K. B. Basseches, wood sculptures from Oaxaca by Moisés Jiménez and Armando Jiménez
(Cinco Puntos, $14.95) 978-1-933693-13-2
Colorful photographs of painted carvings of animals by the Jiménez family in Oaxaca, Mexico, illustrate the alphabet. (3–5)

Big Bug Surprise
written and ill. by Julia Gran
(Scholastic, $12.99) 978-0-439-67609-0
As Prunella saves her classmates and does show and tell, she discusses insects and spiders. Humorous illustrations. (3–5)

★The Busy Little Squirrel
written and ill. by Nancy Tafuri
(S&S, $15.99) 978-0-689-87341-6
Squirrel, busily preparing for winter, does not have time to play with the other animals. Vibrant, full-page watercolor, pen and ink illustrations. (2–5)

Callie Cat, Ice Skater
by Eileen Spinelli, ill. by Anne Kennedy
(Albert Whitman, $16.95) 978-0-8075-1042-1
Callie's experiences with peer pressure and competition lead to a welcome insight into her passion for skating. Lively watercolor illustrations. (3–6)

Can You Growl Like a Bear?
written and ill. by John Butler
(Peachtree, $15.95) 978-1-56145-396-2
Soft, delicate illustrations and easy natural rhyme use animal sounds to create a cozy bedtime atmosphere. (2–5)

Cat Jumped In!
by Tess Weaver, ill. by Emily Arnold McCully
(Clarion, $16) 978-0-618-61488-2
Jumping through an open window, cat creates chaos as he progresses through the house. His eventual triumph is humorously illustrated. (4–7)

A Closer Look
written and ill. by Mary McCarthy
(Greenwillow, $17.89) 978-0-06-124074-4
With bright collages and brief text, this book will stimulate a child's imagination. (3–6)

Digby Takes Charge
by Caroline Jayne Church
(McElderry, $14.99) 978-1-4169-3441-7
A sheepdog gets advice from the farm's pigs and cows on how to handle unruly sheep. Humorous acrylic and collage illustrations. (4–6)

Ⓑ Dog
by Matthew Van Fleet, photos by Brian Stanton
(S&S, $14.99) 978-1-4169-4137-8
Pull tabs enable all kinds of dogs to wag, shake and scratch in this sturdy board book. (2–4)

Dog And Bear: Two Friends Three Stories
written and ill. by Laura Vaccaro Seeger
(Roaring Brook, $12.95) 1-59643-053-2
Bright, simple pictures illuminate funny and tender stories about an unusual friendship. (3–6)

1

Emma's Turtle

by Eve Bunting, ill. by Marsha Winborn
(Boyds Mills, $15.95) 978-1-59078-350-4
Emma's turtle loves to hear about faraway
places and decides to go and see them. (4–6)

The End

by David LaRochelle, ill. by Richard Egielski
(Arthur A. Levine, $16.99) 978-0-439-64011-4
A clever romp which is presented in reverse,
complete with dragons, flying tomatoes and
lots of lemons. Brilliant paintings in explosive
colors. (5–7)

★Every Friday

written and ill. by Dan Yaccarino
(Henry Holt, $16.95) 978-0-8050-7724–7
A small boy and his father share a special
weekly ritual. Gouache illustrations on watercolor paper. (3–6)

Fabian Escapes

written and ill. by Peter McCarty
(Henry Holt, $16.95) 978-0-8050-7713-1
The further adventures of these Caldecott-
winning animals in a story celebrating their
differences. (3–5)

A Family for Old Mill Farm

by Shutta Crum, ill. by Niki Daly
(Clarion, $16) 978-0-618-42846-5
Many possible houses are examined and
claimed by some animals, but only one will do
for a growing family. Lively verse and illustrations. (4–6)

★First the Egg

written and ill. by Laura Vaccaro Seeger
(Roaring Brook, $14.95) 978-1-59643-272-7
Simple text and bold illustration and design
provoke thought about change and creativity.
(4–6)

★Fix It, Sam

by Lori Ries, ill. by Sue Ramá
(Charlesbridge, $15.95) 978-1-57091-598-7
Big brother Sam can always fix his little
brother's mistakes. Delightful colored pencil
illustrations and simple text. (3–6)

Follow The Line
Through The House

written and ill. by Laura Ljungkvist
(Viking, $16.99) 978-0-670-06225-6

A journey through the house with questions
focusing attention on different objects. (3–6)

Fruit

written and ill. by Sara Anderson
(Handprint, $8.95) 978-1-59354-188-0
Vibrant illustrations help distinguish shapes
and colors of common fruits. (2–5)

Global Babies

by Global Fund for Children
(Charlesbridge, $6.95) 978-1-58089-174-5
Striking photographs of babies from around
the world in a board book format. (0–3)

★A Good Day

written and ill. by Kevin Henkes
(Greenwillow, $16.99) 978-0-06-114018-1
Even with disappointment, there is always
hope. Bright, stylized watercolors. (3–5)

Good Morning China

written and ill. by Hu Yong Yi
(Roaring Brook, $16.95) 978-1-59643-240-6
Like bringing a Bruegel to life, the author-
illustrator shows many morning activities and
then combines them into one large foldout
scene. (3–6)

★Has Anyone Seen
My Emily Greene?

by Norma Fox Mazer, ill. by Christine Davenier
(Candlewick, $15.99) 978-0-7636-1384–6
A father-daughter game of hide-and-seek cap-
tured in rhyme and watercolors. (3–5)

How Big Is The World?

written and ill. by Britta Teckentrup
(Boxer Books, $14.95) 978-1-905417-50-6
Little Mole gets many different answers to his
question while traveling far and wide on his
great adventure. Delightful text and energetic,
brightly colored illustrations. (3–6)

How Do You
Make A Baby Smile?

by Philemon Sturges,
ill. by Bridget Strevens-Marzo
(HarperCollins, $17.89) 978-0-06-076073-1
Joyful animals playing with their young turn
out to be baby's stuffed toys. Simple, vibrant
illustrations. (3–5)

I Heard a Little Baa
by Elizabeth MacLeod, ill. by Louise Phillips
(Kids Can Press, $6.95) 978-1-55453-179-0
Bright cartoon-like illustrations and rhyming
text invite readers to guess the hidden animal.
Board book. (2–4)

I'm Dirty!
by Kate & Jim McMullan
(HarperCollins, $16.99) '06 978-0-06-009293-1
A genial backhoe cheerfully does his job of
clearing, chomping and filling. Simple text,
clever typography and exuberant illustrations.
(3–6)

★I'm Going to Grandma's
by Mary Ann Hoberman,
ill. by Tiphanie Beeke
(Harcourt, $16) 978-0-15-216592-5
Sprightly rhymes and colorful acrylics illustrate this story about a special sleepover. (2–5)

"I'm Not Scared!"
written and ill. by Jonathan Allen
(Hyperion, $14.99) 978-0-7868-3722-9
Baby owl insists that she is not scared of the
woods at night. (2–5)

If a Chicken Stayed for Supper
by Carrie Weston, ill. by Sophie Fatus
(Holiday House, $16.95) 978-0-8234-2067-4
Mother Hen brings five little foxes back to
their den and is invited to a special soup din-
ner. Humorous, stylized illustrations. (4–6)

Imagine Harry
by Kate Klise, ill. by M. Sarah Klise
(Harcourt, $16) 978-0-15-205704-6
Little Rabbit goes to school and his imaginary
friend, Harry, eases out of his life. Whimsical
acrylic illustrations. (3–6)

Ivan the Terrier
written and ill. by Peter Catalanotto
(Atheneum, $16.99) 978-1-4169-1247-7
A dog who loves stories keeps interrupting,
until he can star in one. Humorous, lively
illustrations. (3–6)

★Jazz Baby
by Lisa Wheeler, ill. by R. Gregory Christie
(Harcourt, $16) 978-0-15-202522-9
Rhythm and dance fill a baby with joy and love.
Bold, colorful gouache illustrations. (4–6)

★Knuffle Bunny Too: A Case of Mistaken Identity
written and ill. by Mo Willems
(Hyperion, $16.99) 978-1-4231-0299-1
When Trixie eagerly takes her beloved stuffed
bunny to school to show all her friends, she discovers an unpleasant surprise. Hand-drawn ink
sketches overlayed with photographs. (3–5)

Last One in Is a Rotten Egg!
written and ill. by Diane deGroat
(HarperCollins, $15.99) 978-0-06-089294-4
Cousin Wally always has to be first at Easter
until Gilbert teaches him a lesson. Cartoon-
like drawings add to the humor. (4–6)

Leaves
written and ill. by David Ezra Stein
(Putnam, $15.99) 978-0-399-24636-4
A bear cub is dismayed to see the leaves
falling. Many surprises lie in store for him.
Lighthearted illustrations. (3–5)

Leaving the Nest
written and ill. by Mordicai Gerstein
(FSG, $16) 978-0-374-34369-9
A baby blue jay, a girl and a kitten, all eager
to explore, venture from their homes into a
backyard adventure. Sketchy, colorful illustrations. (4–6)

★Little Night
written and ill. by Yuyi Morales
(Roaring Brook, $16.95) 1-59643-088-4
Mother Sky engages in bedtime capers with
her child in this tender loving encounter.
Lyrical pastels. (4–7)

Mama and Little Joe
by Angela McAllister, ill. by Terry Milne
(McElderry, $15.99) 978-1-4169-1631-4
The expensive toys in a household learn an
invaluable lesson when hand-me-down toys
join them. (4–6)

Max Counts His Chickens
written and ill. by Rosemary Wells
(Viking, $15.99) 978-0-670-06222-5
When Max and his sister Ruby search the
house for Easter chicks, Ruby seems to have
all the luck. (3–5)

Meerkat Mail

written and ill. by Emily Gravett
(S&S, $17.99) 978-1-4169-3473-8
A meerkat's postcard to his family describes all his close relatives and his yearning for home. Lively pen-and-ink and color illustrations. (4–6)

Mine!

by Mathilde Stein, ill. by Mies van Hout
(Lemniscaat (Boyds Mills), $16.95)
978-1-59078-506-5
Charlotte teaches a young ghost visitor how to share toys, space and friendship in a story that is both light-hearted and moving. (4–6)

Mouse Shapes

written and ill. by Ellen Stoll Walsh
(Harcourt, $16) 978-0-15-206091-6
Cut-paper collages illustrate the engaging story of mice hiding from a scary cat in a concept book celebrating shapes, colors and creativity. (2–5)

My Brother

written and ill. by Anthony Browne
(FSG, $16) 978-0-374-35120-5
A young boy's admiration for his older brother helps him realize his own worth. Simple text and colored pencil illustrations. (3–5)

★My Cat Copies Me

written and ill. by Yoon-duck Kwon
(Kane/Miller, $15.95) 978-1-933605-26-5
The tender relationship between a Korean girl and her cat as they learn from one another about their world. Korean brushwork paintings. (4–6)

My Colors, My World: Mis Colores, Mi Mundo

written and ill. by Maya Christina Gonzalez
(Children's Book, $16.95) 978-0-89239-221-6
Maya finds color and beauty in her everyday world. Luminous paintings. Bilingual text. (4–6)

My Way/A mi manera: A Margaret and Margarita Story

written and ill. by Lynn Reiser
(Greenwillow, $15.99) 978-0-06-084101-0
Margaret and Margarita sometimes like to do things differently, but always like to do them together. Lively watercolors. (4–6)

Oliver Who Would Not Sleep!

by Mara Bergman, ill. by Nick Maland
(Arthur A. Levine, $16.99) 978-0-439-92826-7
Oliver Donnington Rimington-Sneep takes an exciting adventure just before going to sleep. Humorous, cartoonlike illustrations. (2–6)

Olivia Helps with Christmas

written and ill. by Ian Falconer
(Atheneum, $18.99) 978-1-4169-0786-2
Olivia celebrates Christmas with excitement, energy and delightful chaos. Charcoal and gouache illustrations. (3–6)

Only You

by Robin Cruise, ill. by Margaret Chodos-Irvine
(Harcourt, $16) 978-0-15-216604-5
A gentle, multicultural celebration of parents' love for their children. Bold, colorful illustrations. (3–6)

Out of the Egg

written and ill. by Tina Matthews
(HMC, $12.95) 978-0-618-73741-3
Red Hen cannot get the animals to help grow a seed, but her chick provides a different ending for this version of the familiar tale. Japanese woodblocks. (3–5)

Panda Whispers

written and ill. by Mary Beth Owens
(Dutton, $16.99) 978-0-525-47171-4
A father whispers to his daughter at bedtime, and animal parents lull their children to sleep as well. Soft, warm pastels. (3–6)

Penguin

written and ill. by Polly Dunbar
(Candlewick, $15.99) 978-0-7636-3404-9
Ben's new stuffed toy refuses to obey his commands, producing surprising consequences. Simple, outlined drawings in mixed media. (3–6)

Penguins, Penguins, Everywhere!

written and ill. by Bob Barner
(Chronicle, $14.95) 978-0-8118-5664-5
Color collages accompany whimsical verse about penguin habits. Includes list and description of different varieties. (3–5)

Perros! Perros! Dogs! Dogs!: A Story in English and Spanish
by Ginger Foglesong Guy, ill. by Sharon Glick (Greenwillow, $15.99) '06 978-0-06-083574-3 Dogs romp through town depicting opposites in colorful watercolors and black ink. (3–6)

A Piece of Chalk
by Jennifer A. Ericsson, ill. by Michelle Shapiro (Roaring Brook, $16.95) 978-1-59643-057-0 As a young girl draws with her colorful chalk, her eyes open to the world around her. Stylized colorful pastels. (3–5)

Piggy Wiglet
by David L. Harrison, ill. by Karen Stormer Brooks (Boyds Mills, $16.95) 978-1-59078-386-3 In his exuberance, Piglet runs all through the town and returns to see the sun set over his home pen. Joyful watercolor and pencil illustrations. (2–5)

Piglet and Papa
by Margaret Wild, ill. by Stephen Michael King (Abrams, $14.95) 978-0-8109-1476-6 Piglet needs reassurance that her papa loves her. Warm watercolors. (4–6)

Pigs Love Potatoes
by Anika Denise, ill. by Christopher Denise (Philomel, $15.99) 978-0-399-24036-2 Mamma pig boils one more potato each time another hungry pig comes along. Rhyming text with humorous illustrations. (4–6)

Rabbit's Gift
by George Shannon, ill. by Laura Dronzek (Harcourt, $16) 978-0-15-206073-2 Gentle acrylic illustrations accompany this fable about animals sharing. (4–6)

Rainstorm
written and ill. by Barbara Lehman (HMC, $16) 978-0-618-75639-1 A provocative and beautifully illustrated wordless picture book about a boy, a secret tunnel and friendship. (4–6)

★Rainy Day
by Patricia Lakin, ill. by Scott Nash (Dial, $16.99) 978-0-8037-3092-2 The rainy weather does not stop four crocodiles from having a creative day of adventure and fun. Humorous, computer-generated illustrations. (3–5)

Rhinos Who Rescue
written and ill. by Julie Mammano (Chronicle, $13.95) 978-0-8118-5419-1 Heroic rhinos fight fires and rescue flood victims, while introducing readers to wild words. Vibrant, folk-art style watercolors. (4–6)

Roar!
by Margaret Mayo, ill. by Alex Ayliffe (Carolrhoda, $15.95) 978-0-7613-9473-0 Various animal attributes are highlighted in rhythmic text with energetic, brightly colored illustrations. (2–4)

Roar of a Snore
by Marsha Diane Arnold, ill. by Pierre Pratt (Dial, $16.99) '06 0-8037-2936-7 Jack goes in search of the snorer who awakened him. Exuberant rhymes; lighthearted, acrylic illustrations. (3–6)

Sam Tells Stories
by Thierry Robberecht, ill. by Philippe Goossens (Clarion, $12) 978-0-618-73280-7 Sam discovers that he doesn't need to make up wild stories to please his friends and family. Colorful oil paintings. (3–6)

Ⓑ Sports A To Z
by David Diehl (Lark Books, $5.95) 978-1-60059-113-6 An inventive alphabet book teaches sports terminology. Colorful illustrations. Board book. (3–5)

★Stick
written and ill. by Steve Breen (Dial, $16.99) 978-0-8037-3124-0 How much trouble can a young frog encounter when he tries to be independent? Humorous mixed media illustrations. (4–6)

Macky Pamintuan 2007

Taking A Bath With The Dog And Other Things That Make Me Happy

written and ill. by Scott Menchin
(Candlewick, $15.99) 978-0-7636-2919-9
A sad little girl figures out what makes her happy. Simple, energetic illustrations. (4–6)

★This is a Poem that Heals Fish

by Jean-Pierre Siméon, ill. by Olivier Tallec
(Enchanted Lion, $16.95) 978-1-59270-067-7
Through exhaustive exploration, little Arthur learns what constitutes a poem. Splashy watercolors. (5–7)

Trucks Roll!

by George Ella Lyon,
ill. by Craig Frazier
(Atheneum, $14.99) 978-1-4169-2435-7
Verses describe the many things a truck might carry. Bright, colorful illustrations. (2–4)

Tummy Girl

by Roseanne Thong, ill. by Sam Williams
(Henry Holt, $15.95) 0-8050-7609-3
Rhythmic rhymes portray the early years along with colorful charcoal and pastel illustrations. (3–5)

Very Hairy Bear

by Alice Schertle, ill. by Matt Phelan
(Harcourt, $16) 978-0-15-216568-0
Full page pastel and pencil illustrations create a feeling of warmth as bear carries out his seasonal activities. (2–5)

Virginie's Hat

by Dori Chaconas, ill. by Holly Meade
(Candlewick, $16.99) 978-0-7636-2397-5
Unaware of the dangers lurking behind her, Virginie has a great time getting her hat out of a tree. (3–5)

We Are Cousins/Somos Primos

by Diane Gonzales Bertrand,
ill. by Christina E. Rodriguez
(Piñata, $15.95) 978-1-55885-486-4
Gentle humor in both text and illustrations underscores the warmth of a group of first cousins. (4–7)

What Do Parents Do?: (when you're not home)

by Jeanie Franz Ransom, ill. by Cyd Moore
(Peachtree, $16.95) 978-1-56145-409-9
A boy imagines the naughty child-like behavior of his parents when the children are away. Whimsical illustrations. (4–6)

What Will Fat Cat Sit On?

written and ill. by Jan Thomas
(Harcourt, $12.95) 978-0-15-206051-0
Humorous cartoon-like drawings tell the story as fat cat finds the best place to sit. (3–5)

Who Likes Rain?

written and ill. by Wong Herbert Lee
(Henry Holt, $14.95) 978-0-8050-7734-6
Soft, pastel illustrations capture a little girl's discovery of everything she can do in the rain. (3–6)

Who Will Sing a Lullaby?

by Dee Lillegard, ill. by Dan Yaccarino
(Knopf, $15.99) 978-0-375-81573-7
Only one bird succeeds in stilling a crying baby with its lullaby. Lyrical gouache and airbrush illustrations. (3–5)

Who's in the Tub?

by Sylvie Jones
pictures by Pascale Constantin
(Blue Apple, $15.95) 978-1-59354–612-0
Willo's bath routine is humorously unveiled as he shares his tub with various creatures in an unusual colorful format. (2–4)

Yo, Jo!

written and ill. by Rachel Isadora
(Harcourt, $16) 978-0-15-205783-1
Neighbors greet each other in their unique styles. Cheerful collages. (4–6)

FIVE TO NINE

Laura Freeman 2007

ADVENTURE AND MYSTERY

Clorinda Takes Flight
by Robert Kinerk, ill. by Steven Kellogg
(S&S, $16.99) 978-0-689-86864-1
Clorinda wants to fly—so what if she's a cow?
Clever mixed-media illustrations. (5–8)

Kami And The Yaks
by Andrea Stenn Stryer, ill. by Bert Dodson
(Bay Otter Press, $15.95) 978-0-9778961-0-3
Kami, a deaf boy from the Himalayas, alerts
the family about their injured yak, gaining his
father's respect. Realistic watercolors. (6–10)

Max & Maddy and The Chocolate Money Mystery
by Alexander McCall Smith,
ill. by Macky Pamintuan
(Bloomsbury, $9.95) 978-1-59990-036-0
In an exciting chase, a sibling team uses its
detective skills to find a band of thieves. (7–9)

Max & Maddy and the Bursting Balloons Mystery
by Alexander McCall Smith,
ill. by Macky Pamintuan
(Bloomsbury, $9.95) 978-1-59990-035-3
The two young detectives help Mr. Helium
discover who is sabotaging the balloon race.
(7–9)

Midsummer Knight
written and ill. by Gregory Rogers
(Roaring Brook, $16.95) 978-1-56943-183-6
In this wordless adventure, Bear joins forces
with a fairyland cast to defeat a dastardly vil-
lain. Humorous pen-and-ink and color illustrations. (5–8)

To Catch a Burglar
by Mary Casanova, ill. by Omar Rayyan
(Aladdin, P$4.99) 978-0-689-86813-9
The town dogs band together to catch a dangerous criminal. Clever dialogue, with charcoal illustrations. (7–9)

ANIMALS

Danny's First Snow
written and ill. by Leonid Gore
(Atheneum, $16.99) 978-1-4169-1330-6
When young rabbit experiences his first snow-
fall, he finds his environment greatly changed.
Rich acrylic and pastel illustrations. (4–7)

Diary of a Fly
by Doreen Cronin, ill. by Harry Bliss
(HarperCollins, $16.89)
978-0-06-000157-5
Fly joins her friends worm and spider on an
adventure of discovery and fun. (6–8)

Dog Diaries: Secret Writings Of The Woof Society
by Betsy Byars, Betsy Duffey and
Laurie Myers, ill. by Erik Brooks
(Henry Holt, $15.95) 978-0-8050-7957-9
Dog storytellers gather to share adventures,
real and imagined, about ancient Egypt, Mt.
Vesuvius and the California Gold Rush. (5–8)

Five Nice Mice
written and ill. by Chisato Tashiro, trans. by
Sayako Uchida and Kate Westerlund
(Penguin, $16.99) 978-0-698-40058-0
The frogs won't share their music, so the mice
make their own. Fine, detailed illustrations.
(5–7)

Goodnight Sweet Pig
by Linda Bailey, ill. by Josée Masse
(Kids Can, $16.95) 978-1-55337-844-0
A simple counting book with humorous illustrations and engaging rhymes about a child's
desire to go to sleep. (4–7)

...ANIMALS

★Some Dog!

by Mary Casanova, ill. by Ard Hoyt
(FSG, $16) 978-0-374-37133-3
When an energetic stray dog invades George's peaceful existence and charms his owners, George proves he is still special. Humorous illustrations. (5–7)

The Tale of Pale Male: A True Story

written and ill. by Jeanette Winter
(Harcourt, $16) 978-0-15-205972-9
A pair of red-tailed hawks come into conflict with Manhattan apartment dwellers. Enhancing, colorful illustrations. Based on a true episode. (6–9)

White Owl, Barn Owl

by Nicola Davies, ill. by Michael Foreman
(Candlewick, $16.99) 978-0-7636-3364-6
Watercolors and pastels illustrate this adventure shared by a little girl and her grandfather. (5–8)

BEGINNING READERS

Abracadabra!: Magic with Mouse and Mole

written and ill. by Wong Herbert Yee
(HMC, $15) 978-0-618-75926-2
Mole is very disappointed with a magician's tricks until mouse shows him the magic that surrounds them everyday. Small charcoal and gouache illustrations. (6–8)

At Home in a New Land

written and ill. by Joan Sandin
(HarperCollins, $16.89) 978-0-06-058078-0
When Carl Erik comes to Minnesota from Sweden with his family, he encounters many challenges as a new immigrant. Realistic illustrations. (6–8)

Bones and the Birthday Mystery

by David A. Adler,
ill. by Barbara Johansen Newman
(Viking, $13.99) 978-0-670-06164-8
On the way to Grandpa's birthday party, his present disappears. Can Jeffrey use his detective skills to find it? (6–8)

Cowgirl Kate and Cocoa: School Days

by Erica Silverman, ill. by Betsy Lewin
(Harcourt, $15) 978-0-15-205378-9
Now that Kate is going to school and making new friends, will she still love Cocoa? (6–8)

Custard Surprise

by Bernard Lodge, ill. by Tim Bowers
(HarperCollins, $16.89) 978-0-06-073688-0
Two chickens discover just how smart you have to be to survive in the restaurant business. (5–8)

ELEPHANT AND PIGGIE

★I Am Invited to a Party!

★My Friend Is Sad

★There Is a Bird on Your Head!

★Today I Will Fly!

written and ill. by Mo Willems
(Hyperion, $8.99) 978-1-4231-0687-6, 978-1-4231-0297-7, 978-1-4231-0686-9, 978-1-4231-0295-3
Two best friends share their deep feelings through simple and sincere actions. Humorous, cartoonish illustrations. (4–8)

Follow Me, Mittens

by Lola M. Schaefer,
ill. by Susan Kathleen Hartung
(HarperCollins, $15.99) 978-0-06-054665-6
An eager kitten follows a butterfly—but what happens when the butterfly flies away? (4-7)

Horrible Harry Cracks The Code

by Suzy Kline, ill. by Frank Remkiewicz
(Viking, $13.99) 978-0-670-06200-3
The second best detective in the world must maintain his reputation by learning more about math in order to solve a mystery. (6–8)

The Luck of the Irish

by Margaret McNamara, ill. by Mike Gordon
(Aladdin, $3.99) 978-1-4169-1539-3
Can Katie and her teacher both be right about shamrocks? (6–8)

Max & Mo Go Apple Picking

by Patricia Lakin, ill. by Brian Floca
(Aladdin, $3.99) 978-1-4169-2535-4
Tired of their diet of corn, Max and Mo discover a way to add apple bits and apple sauce to their diet—and even invent an art project. (4–6)

Max & Mo's First Day At School
by Patricia Lakin, ill. by Brian Floca
(Aladdin, P$3.99) 978-1-4169-2533-0
Two hamsters need nametags so that big people in the art room can identify them. Expressive, humorous watercolors. (5–7)

Pip Squeak
by Sarah Weeks, ill. by Jane Manning
(HarperCollins, $16.89) 978-0-06-075637-6
Poor Pip Squeak! He worked so hard to clean his house and then his messy friend, Max, appeared. (5–7)

There Was an Old Lady Who Swallowed Fly Guy
written and ill. by Tedd Arnold
(Scholastic, $5.99) 978-0-439-63906-4
Fly Guy returns, and this time he runs into a fly's worst nightmare: a swallowing old lady! (5–8)

Wiggle and Waggle
by Caroline Arnold, ill. by Mary Peterson
(Charlesbridge, $12.95) 978-1-58089-306-0
Wiggle and Waggle have a wonderful wormy time wriggling through the garden and helping plants grow. (6–8)

FANTASY

The Elves and the Shoemaker
retold by John Cech, ill. by Kirill Chelushkin
(Sterling, $14.95) 978-1-4027-3067-2
A faithful retelling of the classic fairy tale of the struggling shoemaker who receives magical help. Delicate, whimsical illustrations. (5–7)

Fiona's Luck
by Teresa Bateman, ill. by Kelly Murphy
(Charlesbridge, $15.95) 978-1-57091-651-9
Fiona tricks the leprechaun king, who has hoarded the luck of the Irish, into giving some back. (6–9)

Good Enough to Eat
written and ill. by Brock Cole
(FSG, $16) 978-0-374-32737-8
A poor girl who has nothing outwits an ogre and saves herself. Humorous watercolors. (5–7)

Iggy Peck, Architect
by Andrea Beaty, ill. by David Roberts
(Abrams, $15.95) 978-0-8109-1106-2
Iggy Peck's interest in architecture is squashed by a teacher, but is rekindled soon after. Stylized watercolor illustrations. (5–7)

Laura Freeman 2007

The Jewel Box Ballerinas
by Monique de Varennes, pictures by Ana Juan
(S&W, $16.99) 978-0-375-83605-3
A lonely rich woman buys an enchanted music box and learns the power of love. Humorous, colorful acrylic and crayon illustrations. (5–8)

Lionel and the Book of Beasts
by E. Nesbit, retold and ill. by Michael Hague
(HarperCollins, $16.99)
'06 978-0-688-14006–9
A very young King cannot resist opening a magic book. Detailed illustrations recreate the imaginary kingdom. (5–7)

★Pretty Salma: A Little Red Riding Hood Story from Africa
written and ill. by Niki Daly
(Clarion, $16) 978-0-618-72345-4
Little Red Riding Hood is set in Ghana, with interesting variations and colorful, amusing illustrations. (5–8)

The Witch's Child
by Arthur Yorinks, ill. by Jos. A. Smith
(Abrams, $16.95) 978-0-8109-9349-5
A horrible witch creates a child from scraps, but can't bring her to life. Colorful, eerie illustrations. (6–9)

FOLK AND FAIRY TALES

Even Higher
written and ill. by Richard Ungar
(Tundra, $18.95) 978-0-88776-758-6
Every year the rabbi of Nemirov disappears the day before the Jewish New Year. Where does he go? Watercolor and pencil illustrations. (6–8)

...FOLK AND FAIRY TALES

★Glass Slipper, Gold Sandal: A Worldwide Cinderella
by Paul Fleischman, ill. by Julie Paschkis
(Henry Holt, $16.95) 978-0-8050-7953-1
A retelling with a global spin of the classic
Cinderella story is accompanied by colorful,
stylized gouaches. (6–8)

Legend of the Chinese Dragon
by Marie Sellier, ill. by Catherine Louis, callig-
raphy and chop marks by Wang Fei,
trans. by Sibylle Kazeroid
(North-South, $15.95) 978-0-7358-2152-1
The legend of the animal that symbolizes of
peace and joy is presented with expressive
woodblock prints. (6–10)

Little Red Riding Hood
retold and ill. by Jerry Pinkney
(Little, $16.99) 978-0-316-01355-0
Richly colored, expressive illustrations enliven
the traditional tale of the little girl and the
hungry wolf. (5–8)

The Luck of the Loch Ness Monster: A Tale of Picky Eating
by A. W. Flaherty, ill. by Scott Magoon
(HMC, $16) 978-0-618-55644-1
A small worm grows larger and larger feasting
on cast-off food. Pen and digital color illustrations. (4–7)

Martina the Beautiful Cockroach: A Cuban Folktale
retold by Carmen Agra Deedy,
ill. by Michael Austin
(Peachtree, $16.95) 978-1-56145-399-3
Martina uses her grandmother's sage advice to
determine which suitor she will marry. Lavish
acrylic illustrations. (5–9)

Mee-Ann And The Magic Serpent
written and ill. by Baba Wagué Diakité
(Groundwood, $16.95) 978-0-88899-719-7
A vain young girl discovers that looks can be
deceiving. Illustrated with paintings on glazed
tile. (5–7)

Paul Bunyan's Sweetheart
by Marybeth Lorbiecki, ill. by Renée Graef
(Sleeping Bear, $16.95) 978-1-58536-289-9
Paul Bunyan meets his match in Lucette, but
learns that winning her love won't be easy.
(6–9)

The Pen That Pa Built
by David Edwards, ill. by Ashley Wolff
(Tricycle, $14.95) 978-1-58246-153-3
From shearing to weaving—the process of
creating a wool blanket detailed in a cumulative rhyme. Colorful illustrations.(4–7)

Priceless Gifts: A Folktale from Italy
by Martha Hamilton, and Mitch Weiss,
ill. by John Kanzler
(August House, $16.95) 978-0-87483-788-9
A traditional Italian tale, in which ingenuity is
rewarded and greed is punished, is illustrated
with humorous paintings. (6–10)

The Princess And The Pea
written and ill. by Rachel Isadora
(Putnam, $16.99) 978-0-399-24611-1
The classic tale about testing the princess is
set in Africa and illustrated with oils on pat-
terned paper. (4–6)

Red Butterfly: How a Princess Smuggled the Secret of Silk Out of China
by Deborah Noyes, ill. by Sophie Blackall
(Candlewick, $16.99) 978-0-7636-2400-2
A child bride, reluctantly leaving for a distant
kingdom, wants to bring a talisman with her.
Chinese ink and watercolor illustrations. (6–8)

The Rich Man and the Parrot
retold by Suzan Nadimi, ill. by Ande Cook
(Albert Whitman,$16.95) 978-0-8075-5059-5
In this retelling of a thirteenth-century Persian
folktale, a parrot tricks a wealthy merchant.
(6–9)

The Story of Giraffe
conceived and ill. by Guido Pigni,
words by Ronald Hermsen
(Front Street, $16.95) 978-1-932425–87-1
The giraffe's quest to find a mate to board
Noah's Ark meets with success. Simple pastel
illustrations. (5–7)

★Sugar Cane: A Caribbean Rapunzel

by Patricia Storace, pictures by Raúl Colón
(Jump At The Sun, $16.99) 978-0-7868-0791-8
With lush illustrations and appropriate art, the classic folktale has been completely transformed to fit its setting. (7–10)

Wolf! Wolf!

written and ill. by John Rocco
(Hyperion, $15.99) 978-1-4231-0012-3
When a Japanese boy cries "Wolf!" an old wolf thinks he is being invited to lunch. An unusual adaptation with intriguing illustrations. (7–9)

GROWING UP

★And What Comes After a Thousand?

written and ill. by Anette Bley
(Kane/Miller, $15.95) 978-1-933605-27-2
Lisa discovers that her old friend lives on in the memories of all they shared. Dramatic, vibrantly colored illustrations. (6–9)

Being Teddy Roosevelt

by Claudia Mills, ill. by R. W. Alley
(FSG, $16) 978-0-374-30657-1
Inspired by a biography of Teddy Roosevelt, Riley finds clever ways to solve his problems. (7–9)

★The Boy Who Was Raised by Librarians

by Carla Morris, ill. by Brad Sneed
(Peachtree, $16.95) 978-1-56145-391-7
Melvin has great fun growing up with a little help from his favorite people—three zany librarians. Energetic watercolor and gouache illustrations. (6–8)

★Fred Stays with Me!

by Nancy Coffelt, ill. by Tricia Tusa
(Little, $16.99) 978-0-316–88269-9
A little girl shuttles between her divorced parents' homes with an ill-behaved dog. Graceful, tender watercolors. (6–8)

Granddad's Fishing Buddy

by Mary Quigley, ill. by Stéphane Jorisch
(Dial, $16.99) 978-0-8037-2942-1
Sara is in for a surprise when she accompanies her grandfather on a fishing trip. Lyrical watercolors. (5–7)

Hair For Mama

by Kelly A. Tinkham, ill. by Amy June Bates
(Dial, $16.99) 978-0-8037-2955-1
When chemotherapy causes Mama to avoid the annual family photofest, Marcus decides to offer his own hair. Loving illustrations. (5–8)

Jamie and Angus Together

by Anne Fine, ill. by Penny Dale
(Candlewick, $15.99) 978-0-7636-3374-5
A boy and his favorite toy share adventures and survive an attempt at separation. Whimsical pencil illustrations. (5–7)

Lily Brown's Paintings

by Angela Johnson, ill. by E.B. Lewis
(Orchard, $16.99) 978-0-439-78225–8
Lily paints her world in both fantastic and real ways-and it is always wondrous. (4–8)

Lissy's Friends

written and ill. by Grace Lin
(Viking, $15.99) 978-0-670-06072-6
The shy new girl at school makes origami friends—and then real ones. (5–9)

Little Rat Makes Music

by Monika Bang-Campbell, ill. by Molly Bang
(Harcourt, $15) 978-0-15-205305-5
After many trials and tribulations, Little Rat discovers that "practice makes perfect" as she learns how to play the violin. (6–8)

★Mama's Saris

by Pooja Makhijani, ill. by Elena Gomez
(Little, $16.99) 978-0-316-01105-1
A little girl's desire to wear a sari on her seventh birthday offers a glimpse into Indian culture. Vibrant acrylics. (5–8)

Moxy Maxwell Does Not Love Stuart Little

by Peggy Gifford, photos by Valorie Fisher
(S&W, $12.99) 978-0-375–83915-3
Moxy is too busy being an aquatic star to read her school-assigned summer book. (7–10)

Laura Freeman 2007

Nana's Big Surprise: Nana, ¡Qué Sorpresa!
by Amada Irma Pérez,
ill. by Maya Christina Gonzalez
(Children's Book Press, $16.95)
978-0-89239-190-5
When their grandfather dies, a loving Mexican family invites their grandmother to visit. Bilingual text and bold acrylics. (5–8)

A Night of Tamales & Roses
by Joanna H. Kraus,
pictures by Elena Caravela
(Shenanigan Books, $15.95)
978-0-97266-14-4-7
A little flower girl gets the jitters, but is forgiven by her sister, the bride. Realistic oil on canvas illustrations. (6–8)

Piano Piano
by Davide Cali, ill. by Eric Heliot
(Charlesbridge, $15.95) 978-1-58089-191-2
Practice, practice practice. Marcolino's Mom wants him to become a grand pianist, but he has other plans. (5–7)

Pictures From Our Vacation
written and ill. by Lynne Rae Perkins
(Greenwillow, $17.89) 978-0-06-085098-2
A family trip to meet grandparents at an old farmhouse comes alive with honesty and humor. Detailed pen-and-ink and watercolor illustrations. (6–10)

Pitching in for Eubie
by Jerdine Nolen, ill. by E. B. Lewis
(Amistad, $16.99) 978-0-688-14917-8
When her big sister needs extra money for college expenses, Lily finds a way to help. Sensitive watercolors. (5–8)

★Sallie Gal and the Wall-a-kee Man
by Sheila P. Moses, ill. by Niki Daly
(Scholastic, $15.99) 978-0-439-90890-0
Sallie Gal's desire for colorful ribbons helps her appreciate her rural southern neighborhood's daily life and her mother's integrity. (6–9)

The Tale of Pip and Squeak
written and ill. by Kate Duke
(Dutton, $16.99) 978-0-525-47777-8
Pip paints, Squeak sings, and each drives the other nuts. Can the mouse brothers learn to live together? Cheerful, detailed watercolor and gouache illustrations. (4–8)

Ten Ways to Make My Sister Disappear
by Norma Fox Mazer
(Arthur A. Levine, $16.99) 978-0-439-83983-9
Will events split ten-year-old Spring and her bossy older sister further apart . . . or bring them closer together? (7–10)

HUMOR

17 Things I'm Not Allowed to Do Anymore
by Jenny Offill, ill. by Nancy Carpenter
(S & W, $15.99) 978-0-375-83596-4
Glue, paste, lies and pranks: a little girl has lots of ideas that get her in trouble. Amusing pen, ink and digitally produced illustrations. (6–8)

Aunt Nancy and The Bothersome Visitors
by Phyllis Root, ill. by David Parkins
(Candlewick, $16.99) 978-0-7636-3074-4
Aunt Nancy outwits a number of troublemakers in this delightful anthology of trickster stories. A great read-aloud. (6–9)

Beauty and the Beaks: A Turkey's Cautionary Tale
by Mary Jane Auch,
ill. by Mary Jane Auch and Herm Auch
(Holiday House, $16.95) 978-0-8234-1990-6
Lance is enjoying his invitation to the feast—until Beauty discovers he's going to be the feast! Hilarious egg-centric computerized illustrations. (6–8)

★Big Bad Wolves At School
by Stephen Krensky, ill. by Brad Sneed
(S&S, $15.99) 978-0-689-83799-9
Rufus, a young, active wolf, struggles to fit in at school until his classmates recognize the value of his abilities. Lively, funny illustrations. (4–8)

Boris Ate A Thesaurus

by Neil Steven Klayman, ill. by Barry M. Chung
(Rainbow Bridge, $14.95) 978-1-60095-258-6
A young boy starts speaking in synonyms after swallowing a thesaurus. Cartoon-like illustrations. (5–8)

The Cheese

by Margie Palatini, ill. by Steve Johnson, and Lou Fancher
(HarperCollins, $17.89) 978-0-06-052631-3
A cumulative adaptation of "The Farmer in the Dell" is sparked by silly watercolors. (6–9)

★The Chicken-Chasing Queen of Lamar County

by Janice N. Harrington, ill. by Shelley Jackson
(FSG, $16) 978-0-374-31251-0
Living on a farm with her grandmother, a young African-American girl sets out to catch Miss Hen until she realizes the chicken has a secret. Exuberant collages. (5–8)

Dexter Bexley and the Big Blue Beastie

written and ill. by Joel Stewart
(Holiday House, $16.95) 978-0-8234-2068-1
Young Dexter needs to keep a bored monster from considering him a tasty morsel. Colorful watercolors. (5–7)

★Do Unto Otters: A Book About Manners

written and ill. by Laurie Keller
(Henry Holt, $16.95) 978-0-8050-7996-8
Mr. Rabbit, suspicious of his new neighbors, learns that practicing the Golden Rule can win friends. Colorful acrylics depict comical characters. (5–8)

Dolores Meets Her Match

written and ill. by Barbara Samuels
(FSG, $16) 978-0-374-31758-4
Dolores learns how to share the spotlight and to accept her cat as he is. Delightful illustrations. (6–8)

Flat Stanley

by Jeff Brown, ill. by Scott Nash
(HarperCollins, $16.99) '06 978-0-06-112904-9
Crushed by a bulletin board, Stanley is flat and can be mailed to all kinds of places. Newly illustrated in color and with a larger format. (5–8)

Gimme Cracked Corn and I Will Share

written and ill. by Kevin O'Malley
(Walker, $16.95) 978-0-8027-9684-4
Puns and wacky humorous text enliven a chicken's quest for cracked corn. Pen and ink and watercolor illustrations. (7–10)

Ginger Bear

written and ill. by Mini Grey
(Knopf, $15.99) 978-0-375-84253-5
Share the adventures of an unusually resourceful cookie. Humorous, detailed illustrations. (5–7)

★Heat Wave

by Eileen Spinelli, ill. by Betsy Lewin
(Harcourt, $16) 978-0-15-216779-0
Before home air conditioners, residents of a small town find creative ways to deal with a sweltering heat wave. Engaging brush and ink illustrations. (6–8)

How the Ladies Stopped the Wind

by Bruce McMillan,
ill. with paintings by Gunnella
(HMC, $16) 978-0-618-77330-5
Women in an Icelandic village decide to plant trees to stop the wind, but the sheep think otherwise. Oil paintings in folk art style. (5–8)

★I'd Really Like To Eat A Child

by Sylviane Donnio,
ill. by Dorothée de Monfried
(Random, $14.99) 978-0-375-83761-6
A very young crocodile learns that good nutrition is the secret to growing and realizing his dream—to eat a child. Humorous illustrations, (5–9)

Mercy Watson: Princess In Disguise

by Kate DiCamillo, ill. by Chris Van Dusen
(Candlewick, $12.99) 978-0-7636-3014-0
Mercy, the beloved porcine pet of the Watsons, thoroughly enjoys Halloween once she realizes that it involves treats and a good chase! (5–8)

Mokie & Bik

by Wendy Orr, ill. by Jonathan Bean
(Henry Holt, $15.95) 978-0-8050-7979-1
A twin sister and brother live on a boat and get into all sorts of humorous scrapes. (5–7)

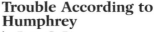

FIVE TO NINE

A Porc In New York
written and ill. by Catherine Stock
(Holiday House, $16.95) 978-0-8234-1994-4
Some French farm animals invade New York
City, followed by their owner and his dog.
Amusing, detailed watercolors. (6–8)

Pssst!
written and ill. by Adam Rex
(Harcourt, $16) 978-0-15-205817-3
Zoo animals devise ways to use the objects
they request of a young visitor. Ingenious text
and humorous illustrations. (6–9)

The Real Story of Stone Soup
by Ying Chang Compestine,
ill. by Stéphane Jorisch
(Dutton, $16.99) 978-0-525-47493-7
Set in China, this traditional story of creating
a delicious dish out of local ingredients is
given a fanciful twist. (5–8)

Soupy Saturdays with the Pain and the Great One
by Judy Blume, ill. by James Stevenson
(Delacorte, $12.99) 978-0-385-73305-2
The first- and third-grade siblings are back
with their bristly relationship and humorous
antics. Black-and-white illustrations, full of
character. (6–9)

★The Talented Clementine
by Sara Pennypacker, ill. by Marla Frazee
(Hyperion, $14.99) 978-0-7868-3870-7
In a series of hilarious mishaps, an irrepress-
ible girl discovers her value to the school talent show. (6–9)

That Rabbit Belongs to Emily Brown
by Cressida Cowell, ill. by Neal Layton
(Hyperion, $16.99) 978-14231-0645-6
Naughty Queen Gloriana gets a well-deserved
lesson in how to make her teddy bear love-
able. Sketchy watercolors. (6–8)

Trouble According to Humphrey
by Betty G. Birney
(Putnam, $14.99) 978-0-399-24505-3
When Room 26 created a model town, who
knew that it would lead to trouble for
Humphrey the hamster? (6–10)

Two Sticks
by Orel Protopopescu, ill. by Anne Wilsdorf
(FSG, $16) 978-0-374-38022-9
Maybelle just has to drum with her "tried and
trusty true sticks." A humorous, rhyming
bayou adventure. (6–8)

★Waking Up Wendell
by April Stevens, ill. by Tad Hills
(S&W, $15.99) 978-0-375–83621-3
One little bird at #1 Fish Street triggers a
domino effect that wakes up each house in the
morning. Humorous illustrations. (5–8)

When Dinosaurs Came with Everything
by Elise Broach, ill. by David Small
(Atheneum, $16.99) 978-0-689-86922-8
Enormous reptiles turn out to be friends and
helpers when they follow a small boy home.
Joyful watercolor and ink illustrations. (5–8)

Whopper Cake
by Karma Wilson, and Will Hillenbrand
(McElderry, $16.99) 978-0-689-83844-6
Grandpa's love for cooking is as tremendous
as the cake he makes for grandma. Exuberant
ink and tempera illustrations. (4–7)

The Wicked Big Toddlah
written and ill. by Kevin Hawkes
(Knopf, $16.99) 978-0-375–82427-2
This young Mainer is one big baby! Hilarious
and clever illustrations. (5–7)

PAST

Anne Hutchinson's Way
by Jeannine Atkins, ill. by Michael Dooling
(FSG, $17) 978-0-374-30365-5
In seventeenth-century Massachusetts, a brave
woman refuses to obey the Puritan minister.
Strong, realistic oil paintings. (6–9)

Laura Freeman 2007

The Buffalo Storm
by Katherine Applegate, ill. by Jan Ormerod
(Clarion, $16) 978-0-618-53597-2
Lyrical language and vibrant watercolors
evoke the fears and courageousness of a
young pioneer girl on the Oregon Trail. (5–8)

Dadblamed Union Army Cow
by Susan Fletcher,
ill. by Kimberly Bulcken Root
(Candlewick, $16.99) 978-0-7636-2263-3
Taking a cow to war isn't easy—but she may
have saved these Union soldiers' lives. Based
on a true story. (7–9)

Dolley Madison
Saves George Washington
written and ill. by Don Brown
(HMC, $16) 978-0-618-41199-3
In 1812 with the British advancing, Dolley
Madison pauses to save important papers and
the Gilbert Stuart portrait of our first president. (6–9)

The Escape of Oney Judge:
Martha Washington's Slave
Finds Freedom
written and ill. by Emily Arnold McCully
(FSG, $16) 978-0-374-32225-0
A slave escapes the household of President
and Martha Washington to live as a free
woman. Expressive watercolors. (7–10)

Ghost Ship
by Mary Higgins Clark, ill. by Wendell Minor
(S&S, $17.99) 978-1-4169-3514-8
A relic from the past leads Thomas to delve
into the history of his grandmother's Cape
Cod house and the sea captain who once lived
in it. (5–7)

Helen, Ethel & the Crazy Quilt:
Based on the 1890 Letters
Between Helen Keller
and Ethel Orr
by Nancy Orr Johnson Jensen,
ill. by Dawn Peterson
(Mayhaven Publishing, $23.95)
978-1-93227810-1
Two ten-year-olds, Helen Keller and Ethel
Orr, develop a friendship through letters.
Archival photographs, watercolors and actual
artifacts enhance the tale. (7–10)

Junk Man's Daughter
by Sonia Levitin, ill. by Guy Porfirio
(Sleeping Bear, $17.95) 978-1-58536-315-5
Warm gentle paintings enhance this tale of an
immigrant family's struggle to succeed in
America. (6–9)

Once Upon a Full Moon
by Elizabeth Quan
(Tundra, $19.95) 978-0-88776-813-2
The journey of the Lee King family from
Canada to China in the 1920s. Precisely delin-
eated watercolors. (7–10)

One Thousand Tracings:
Healing the Wounds
of World War II
written and ill. by Lita Judge
(Hyperion, $15.99) 978-1-4231-0008-9
A moving memoir of the author's grandparents' generosity to German civilian survivors
of World War II. Strong watercolor illustrations along with collages of photos and letters.
(6–10)

The Orange Shoes
by Trinka Hakes Noble, ill. by Doris Ettlinger
(Sleeping Bear, $16.95) 978-1-58536-277-6
A young girl uses her artistic talent and ingenuity to overcome the cruelty of classmates
and to help her school. (7–9)

Pennies in a Jar
by Dori Chaconas, ill. by Ted Lewin
(Peachtree, $16.95) 978-1-56145-422-8
Getting over your fears is hard—especially
when your dad's away at war. Expressive
watercolors. (7–9)

A Picture for Marc
by Eric A. Kimmel, ill. by Matthew Trueman
(Random, $11.99) 978-0-375–83253-6
A fictionalized glimpse of artist Marc Chagall,
whose Russian parents are reluctant to accept
his dream of becoming an artist. (7–9)

★Seeing the Elephant:
A Story of the Civil War
by Pat Hughes, ill. by Ken Stark
(FSG, $16) 978-0-374-38024-3
Ten-year-old Izzie yearns to contribute to the
Union cause but finds that war is neither glo-
rious nor one-sided. Realistic oil paintings.
(7–10)

Terrible Storm

by Carol Otis Hurst, ill. by S. D. Schindler
(Greenwillow, $16.99) 978-0-06-009001-2
During the blizzard of 1888, two young men
get stuck for days in unpleasant situations.
Watercolor and black ink illustrations. (5–7)

Vinnie and Abraham

by Dawn FitzGerald, ill. by Catherine Stock
(Charlesbridge, $15.95) 978-1-57091-658-8
Vinnie Ream fights for her dream and
becomes the sculptor of the statue of
Abraham Lincoln which stands in the Capitol
rotunda. (7–10)

When I Met the Wolf Girls

by Deborah Noyes, ill. by August Hall
(HMC, $17) 978-0-618-60567-5
In her Indian orphanage in the 1920s, seven-
year-old Bulu writes about the behavior of two
girls who have been raised in the jungle by
wolves. Acrylic paintings. (7–9)

When the Shadbush Blooms

by Carla Messinger, with Susan Katz,
ill. by David Kanietakeron Fadden
(Tricycle, $15.95) 978-1-58246-192-2
On side-by-side pages indicating past and
present, the Lenape cycle of seasons is
described by Native Americans. Expressive
acrylic paintings. (6–8)

★Wind Flyers

by Angela Johnson, ill. by Loren Long
(S&S, $16.99) 978-0-689-84879-7
A great-great uncle talks to his young nephew
about his love of flight and his experiences as
a Tuskegee Airman during World War II.
(6–9)

Casey Back at Bat

by Dan Gutman, ill. by Steve Johnson, and
Lou Fancher
(HarperCollins, $16.99) 978-0-06-056025-6
The famous batter tries again in this imagina-
tive sequel to the familiar poem. Period paint-
ings and collages. (6–8)

Laura Freeman 2007

Tennis Anyone?

written and ill. by Shane McG
(Carolrhoda, $15.95) 978-0-8225-6901-5
What is Tom supposed to do with a tennis
racquet? It doesn't beep or crash or whirr—
and who plays tennis? Cartoon-like illustrations. (6–8)

Always Come Home to Me

written and ill. by Belle Yang
(Candlewick, $16.99) 978-0-7636-2899-4
Young twins living in China try to retrieve
their beloved doves who were given to their
uncle. Bright, gouache illustrations. (6–9)

Angelina's Island

written and ill. by Jeanette Winter
(FSG, $16) 978-0-374-30349-5
During Brooklyn's West African Day Parade,
Angelina learns that home is where the heart
is. A colorful ode to Jamaica. (5–7)

Armando and the Blue Tarp School

by Edith Hope Fine, and Judith Pinkerton
Josephson, ill. by Hernán Sosa
(Lee & Low, $16.95) 978-1-58430-278-0
In a semi-biographical telling, a teacher in a
poor Mexican neighborhood inspires his stu-
dents to learn. Watercolor and ink illustrations. (6–8)

The Bad Luck Chair

by Sue Wilkowski, ill. by CB Decker
(Dutton, $15.99) 978-0-525-47794-5
Fourth-grader Addy must overcome bad luck
and her own shyness as she struggles to free
her school from a curse. (7–10)

Best Friend Emma
by Sally Warner, ill. by Jamie Harper
(Viking, $14.99) 978-0-670-06173-0
Eight-year-old Emma decides that the new girl will be her best friend, forgetting that she already has Annie Pat. Black-and-white illustrations. (7–10)

Bravo, Tavo!
by Brian Meunier, ill. by Perky Edgerton
(Dutton, $16.99) 978-0-525-47478-4
A poor Mexican farmer and his basketball-loving son both fulfill their dreams after they uncover an ancient irrigation system. (6–9)

★Cherry Time
written and ill. by Daniela Bunge
(Minedition, $16.99) 978-0-698-40057-3
A shy boy overcomes his fears with the help of a dog and a new friend. Dramatic illustrations. (5–8)

Gooney the Fabulous
by Lois Lowry, ill. by Middy Thomas
(HMC, $15) 978-0-618—76691-8
Aesop's fables inspire Gooney Bird Greene and her second-grade classmates to create their own animal fables, with delightful results. (5–8)

★Grandfather's Wrinkles
by Kathryn England, ill. by Richard McFarland
(Flashlight, $15.95) 978-0-9729225-9-3
A tender tale of Lucy's relationship with her grandfather who shares his memories with her. Colored pencil, watercolor and pastel illustrations. (6–10)

Hair Dance!
by Dinah Johnson, photos by Kelly Johnson
(Henry Holt, $16.95) 978-0-8050-6523-7
Charming photographs and a brief text illustrate the wonders of little girls' hair styles. (5–8)

I Remember Abuelito: A Day of the Dead Story
by Janice Levy, ill. by Loretta Lopez, Spanish trans. by Miguel Arisa
(Albert Whitman, P$6.95) 978-0-8075-3516-5
A heartfelt story of a young girl celebrating her recently deceased grandfather on 'The Day of the Dead' in Mexico. Informative art. (6–9)

The John Hancock Club
by Louise Borden, ill. by Adam Gustavson
(McElderry, $16.99) 978-1-4169-1813-4
As Sean and his third-grade classmates master cursive handwriting, they also learn about an important founding father. (6–9)

Lily and the Paper Man
by Rebecca Upjohn, ill. by Renne Benoit
(Second Story Press, $14.95) 978-1-897187-19-7
A little girl develops confidence, pride and empathy by helping a homeless man. Realistic, vibrant watercolors. (6–9)

My Dadima Wears a Sari
by Kashmira Sheth, ill. by Yoshko Jaeggi
(Peachtree, $16.95) 978-1-56145-392-4
Evoking personal memories, a grandmother lovingly shares the many characteristics of a sari with her granddaughter. Fabric-inspired illustrations. (6–9)

★My Little Grandmother Often Forgets
by Reeve Lindbergh, ill. by Kathryn Brown
(Candlewick, $16.99) 978-0-7636-1989-3
Tom's loving relationship with his grandmother, who suffers from memory loss, is tenderly expressed in rhyme. Ink and watercolor illustrations. (4–7)

Nikki and Deja
by Karen English, ill. by Laura Freeman
(Clarion, $15) 978-0-618-75238-6
A new girl in school challenges the friendship between Nikki and Deja. Black-and-white illustrations. (8–10)

★On Meadowview Street
written and ill. by Henry Cole
(Greenwillow, $17.89) 978-0-06-056482-7
When Caroline moves to Meadowview Street, she doesn't see a meadow or a view, but she finds a way to make a change. (5–7)

Oye, Celia!: A Song for Celia Cruz
by Katie Sciurba, ill. by Edel Rodriguez
(Henry Holt, $16.95) 978-0-8050-7468-0
The song "The Queen of Salsa" arouses a Cuban girl's love for her country. Poetic language with powerful, multi-media illustrations. Glossary. (6–9)

The Perfect Gift

written and ill. by Rohan Henry
(Stewart, Tabori & Chang, $8.95)
978-1-58479-658-9
Leo Rabbit finds the perfect gift for his best friend in a most unexpected place. Simple black-and-white line drawings. (6–8)

Phineas L. MacGuire Gets Slimed!

by Frances O'Roark Dowell,
ill. by Preston McDaniels
(Atheneum, $16.99) 978-1-4169-0196–9
When Mac decides to grow molds for his fourth-grade science project, help comes from unexpected places. (7–9)

★The Top Job

by Elizabeth Cody Kimmel,
ill. by Robert Neubecker
(Dutton, $16.99) 978-0-525-47789-1
Changing a light bulb is sometimes more dangerous than it sounds. Amusing illustrations. (6–8)

The Woodcutter's Gift/ El Regalo del Lenador

by Lupe Ruiz-Flores, ill. by Elaine Jerome,
Spanish trans. by Gabriela Baeza Ventura
(Piñata, $15.95) 978-1-55885-489-5
A zoo of colorful, carved animals in a small town is coveted by a museum in a big city. (6–9)

NINE TO TWELVE

Penny Dale 2007

ADVENTURE AND MYSTERY

Camel Rider
by Prue Mason
(Charlesbridge, $15.95) 978-1-58089-314-5
Two boys from two different cultures face the
unrelenting desert together. (9–12)

Elephant Run
by Roland Smith
(Hyperion, $15.99) 978-1-4231-0402-5
Steamy jungles, elephant handlers, a Japanese
invasion and young love make for an exotic
adventure in 1940s Burma. (10–14)

The Faceless Fiend: Being the Tale of a Criminal Mastermind, His Masked Minions and a Princess with a Butter Knife, Involving Explosives and a Certain Amount of Pushing and Shoving
by Howard Whitehouse, ill. by Bill Slavin
(Kids Can, $16.95) 978-1-55453-130-1
Emmaline and Rab must help their friend
Princess Purnah evade the evil clutches of her
enemies. Loads of fun! (10–12)

★The Invention Of Hugo Cabret
written and ill. by Brian Selznick
(Scholastic, $22.99) 978-0-439-81378-5
A twelve-year-old boy uncovers secrets from
the past, told through drawings which alter-
nate with text in silent film style. (8–12)

The Mysterious Benedict Society
by Trenton Lee Stewart, ill. by Carson Ellis
(Little, $16.99) 978-0-316-05777-6
Mr. Benedict has a plan to foil his evil twin's
attempt at mind control. Four gifted children
accept the challenge to help him succeed.
(10–12)

Night of the Howling Dogs
by Graham Salisbury
(Wendy Lamb, $16.99) 978-0-385-73122-5
In a remote spot on the island of Hawaii, a
Boy Scout troop survives an earthquake and a
tsunami. Based on a true incident. (9–12)

Nobody's Princess
by Esther Friesner
(Random, $16.99) 978-0-375-87528-1
A young Spartan princess who will become
Helen of Troy bucks traditional expectations
to choose her own life. (9–13)

Shots at Sea
by Tom Lalicki
(FSG, $15.95) 978-0-374-31679-2
Nate and his famous mentor, Harry Houdini,
must foil an attempt to assassinate the
President Theodore Roosevelt aboard the
Lusitania in 1911. (8–12)

The Theft & the Miracle
by Rebecca Wade
(HarperCollins, $16.99) 978-0-06-077493-6
The mysterious theft of a medieval statue from
Worcester Cathedral launches Hannah on a
thrilling quest for its recovery. (9–12)

Thora And The Green Sea-Unicorn: Another Half-Mermaid Tale
by Gillian Johnson
(HarperCollins, $15.99) 978-0-06-074381-9
When a thief steals ten-year-old Thora's pet
and sinks her family's houseboat, she uses her
brain and her unusual abilities to save the day.
(8–12)

...ADVENTURE AND MYSTERY

The Treasures of Weatherby
by Zilpha Keatley Snyder
(Atheneum, $15.95) 978-1-4169–1398-6
His life complicated by his shortness, twelve-year-old Harleigh tries to foil the plans of a relative seeking the long-lost fortune of his family. (8–12)

ANIMALS

Barbaro: America's Horse
by Shelley Fraser Mickle
(Aladdin, P$8.99) 978-1-4169-4865-0
The young racer won the Kentucky Derby, but lost the game of life after failing to overcome an injury. (9–13)

Little Squire: The Jumping Pony
by Judy Andrekson, ill. by David Parkins
(Tundra, $7.95) 978-0-88776-770-8
In the 1930s, the Irish-born Connemara pony and his rider, Mickey Walsh, weather hard times to become champions in America. (10–14)

FANTASY

At the Firefly Gate
by Linda Newbery
(David Fickling Books, $15.99)
978-0-385-75113-1
In his new community in a British village, twelve-year-old Henry meets people who seem strangely familiar. (9–12)

Darkwing
by Kenneth Oppel, ill. by Keith Thompson
(HarperCollins, $17.89) 978-0-06-085055-5
Unexpected shifts in the food chain and mutations which allow a gliding bat to begin flying, bring chaos and fear to this imagined Paleocene landscape. (12–14)

The Discovery Of Dragons: New Research Revealed
written and ill. by Graeme Base
(Abrams, $19.95) 978-0-8109-5967-5
A series of sophisticated letters provide an amusing parody on the subject of serpentology. Fanciful illustrations. (10–14)

Dragon's Keep
by Janet Lee Carey
(Harcourt, $17) 978-0-15-205926-2
A strangely handicapped princess overcomes adversity through strength of character. Well-crafted. (10–12)

★The Flying Bed: A Magical Adventure
by Nancy Willard, ill. by John Thompson
(Blue Sky, $16.99) 978-0-590-25610-0
Lush paintings of Florence, Italy illumine this superb, modern fairy tale. (8–12)

The Garden of Eve
by K. L. Going
(Harcourt, $17) 978-0-15-205986-6
After her mother's death, Evie uses magic to heal her sadness. (9–11)

The Golden Dream of Carlo Chuchio
by Lloyd Alexander
(Henry Holt, $18.95) 978-0-8050-8333-0
Carlo finds a treasure map and seeks his fortune with a servant, a wise man and a spunky girl as companions in this Arabian Nights tale. (9–12)

Missing Magic
by Emma Laybourn
(Dial, $16.99) 978-0-8037-3219-3
When trouble strikes, eleven-year-old Ned finds out there might be more to lacking magical ability than he realized. (8–11)

The Neddiad: How the Neddie Took the Train, Went to Hollywood and Saved Civilization
by Daniel Pinkwater
(HMC, $16) 978-0-618-59444-3
After Neddie moves from Chicago to Los Angeles, he makes new friends and has strange adventures. (9–11)

One Beastly Beast (Two Aliens, Three Inventors, Four Fantastic Tales)
by Garth Nix, ill. by Brian Biggs
(HarperCollins, $16.89) 978-0-06-084320-5
Four stories in which a boy pursues video pirates; a princess searches for adventure; an inventor longs to be adopted and a girl aids a sea serpent. (10–13)

The Phantom Isles
by Stephen Alter
(Bloomsbury, $16.95) 978-1-58234-738-7
When ghosts are discovered imprisoned in books, Courtney, Orion, Ming and the librarian decide to free them. (9–11)

Samuel Blink And The Forbidden Forest
by Matt Haig
(Putnam, $16.99) 978-0-399-24739-2
Twelve-year-old Samuel defies the mystery and dangers of a Norwegian forest to rescue his sister from threatening creatures. (9–12)

Theodosia and the Serpents of Chaos
by R. L. LaFevers, ill. by Yoko Tanaka
(HMC, $16) 978-0-618-75638-4
Theodosia decides she must save Britain when her archaeologist mother brings home the cursed Heart of Egypt.

The Titan's Curse
by Rick Riordan
(Miramax Books, $17.95) 978-1-4231-0145-1
Percy, a half-child of Poseidon, living in the modern world, now must battle the lord of the Titans. Humor and adventure meet in a contemporary fantasy. (10–13)

What-the-Dickens: The Story of a Rogue Tooth Fairy
by Gregory Maguire
(Candlewick, $15.99) 978-0-7636-2961-8
On an endless storm-ravaged night, and distracted by tales of tooth fairies, three children and their inept but story-loving cousin wait for help. (10–12)

The White Elephant
by Sid Fleischman, ill. by Robert McGuire
(Greenwillow, $15.99) '06 978-0-06-113136-3
A boy crosses paths with a nasty prince, who saddles him with a sacred elephant with a mind of its own. (8–11)

FOLK AND FAIRY TALES

Amaterasu: Return of the Sun: A Japanese Myth
by Paul D. Storrie, photos by Ron Randall
(Graphic Universe, $26.60) 978-0-8225-5968-9
With larger than life comic book style heroes and heroines, the Shinto myth of the goddess of the sun is retold. (8–12)

Beowulf: A Hero's Tale Retold
retold and ill. by James Rumford
(HMC, $17) 978-0-618-75637-7
A new version of the exploits of the Anglo-Saxon warrior tells how he came to defeat the monster Grendel. (9–12)

Beowulf: A Tale of Blood, Heat, and Ashes
retold by Nicky Raven, ill. by John Howe
(Candlewick, $18.99) 978-0-7636-3647-0
This retelling of Beowulf's slaying of Grendel pits a true hero against the most fearsome of monsters. Watercolor, ink and colored pencil illustrations. (8–12)

Rip Van Winkle's Return
by Eric A. Kimmel,
ill. by Leonard Everett Fisher
(FSG, $17) 978-0-374-36308-6
Irving's famous story features a changed ending. Strong acrylic paintings. (8–11)

GROWING UP

★The Aurora County All-Stars
by Deborah Wiles
(Harcourt, $16) 978-0-15-206068-8
In a small town in Mississippi, a hopeful twelve-year-old baseball player must find courage to deal with life and death messages. (9–12)

Being Bee
by Catherine Bateson
(Holiday House, $16.95) 978-0-8234-2104-6
Will having her dad's girlfriend move in with them be as terrible as Bee fears? (9–11)

Penny Dale 2007

★Bird Springs
by Carolyn Marsden
(Viking, $14.99) 978-0-670-06193-8
Gregory learns how to cope with his family's
break-up and the move from their Navaho
reservation. (8–12)

★Brendan Buckley's Universe and Everything in It
by Sundee Tucker Frazier
(Delacorte, $14.99) 978-0-385-73439-4
Biracial ten-year-old Brendan loves scientific
investigation. Can it help him understand why
his Mom will have nothing to do with her
father? (9–12)

Chess Rumble
by G. Neri, art by Jesse Joshua Watson
(Lee & Low, $18.95) 978-1-58430-279-7
After his sister's death and his father's depar-
ture, Marcus fights with everyone and everything until he meets the chess master. (11–13)

★Circle The Truth
by Pat Schmatz
(Carolrhoda, $16.95) 978-0-8225-7268-8
When Rith finds a staircase, he begins to learn
something about his "dead" father, his family
and himself. (9–12)

Diary of a Would-be Princess
by Jessica Green
(Charlesbridge, $15.95) 978-1-58089–1166-0
In contemporary Australia, Jillian finds her
niche with the help of an exceptional teacher
in the world of in-crowds and cliques. (9–12)

Do Not Pass Go
by Kirkpatrick Hill
(McElderry, $15.99) 978-1-4169–11400-6
Initially ashamed when his father is jailed for
drug use, Deet makes discoveries about
prison, his family and himself. (9–14)

Do The Math: Secrets, Lies, And Algebra
by Wendy Lichtman
(Greenwillow, $17.89) 978-0-06-122956-5
Tess uses math to help her solve life's problems, but what happens when there is no right
answer? (10–14)

Edward's Eyes
by Patricia MacLachlan
(Atheneum, $15.99) 978-1-4169-2743-3
Jake's younger brother, Edward, speaks
French and throws a knuckleball. Jake loves
him dearly—and then... (8–11)

Eggs
by Jerry Spinelli
(Little, $15.99) 978-0-316-16646-1
Angry nine-year-old David finds an unlikely
friend in a quirky thirteen-year-old. (9–12)

★Grandfather's Dance
by Patricia MacLachlan
(HarperCollins, $14.99) '06 978-0-06-027560-0
The conclusion to the Witting family's tale of
life on the prairie brings to life the special
qualities of family and the simple reality of
death. (8–10)

How it Happened in Peach Hill
by Marthe Jocelyn
(Wendy Lamb, $15.99) 978-0-375-83701-2
During the early 1920s, a fifteen-year-old
struggles to free herself from her role as assistant in her mother's phony clairvoyant practice. (10–12)

In Jesse's Shoes: Appreciating Kids with Special Needs
by Beverly Lewis, ill. by Laura Nikiel
(Bethany House, $9.99) 978-0-7642-0313-8
Allie is in charge of her older autistic brother.
Although she resents his behavior, she learns
to appreciate his attributes. (9–11)

Kimchi & Calamari
by Rose Kent
(HarperCollins, $15.99) 978-0-06-083769-3
A Korean child, adopted by an Italian-
American family, reaches his teens and begins
to struggle with feelings of alienation. (9–12)

Leap
by Jane Breskin Zalben
(Knopf, $15.99) 978-0-375-83871-2
A serious medical mishap causes Daniel, a
promising swimmer, to lean on his friend
Krista for help. (10–13)

The Lemonade War
by Jacqueline Davies
(HMC, $16) 978-0-618-75043-6
Jessie skips a year and goes into the same fourth-grade class as her older brother! (8–10)

★Little Klein
by Anne Ylvisaker
(Candlewick, $15.99) 978-0-7636-3359-2
Nine-year-old Harold's big brothers always come to the rescue. Will he be able to help them when they get into trouble? (8–11)

Louisiana's Song
by Kerry Madden
(Viking, $16.99) 978-0-670-06153-2
Outspoken and resourceful, twelve-year-old Olivia helps keep her struggling mountain family together after her father's car accident. (9–12)

The Middle Of Somewhere
by J.B. Cheaney
(Knopf, $15.99) 978-0-375-83790-6
A bleak summer turns exciting when twelve-year-old Ronnie and her ADHD little brother tour Kansas in an RV with their "wind prospector" grandfather. (10–12)

My Last Best Friend
by Julie Bowe
(Harcourt, $16) 978-0-15-205777-0
Ida May struggles valiantly with losing her best friend and the challenge of finding a new one. (8–10)

★Robot Dreams
written and ill. by Sara Varon
(First Second, $16.95) 978-1-59643-108-9
The love and agony of a new friendship between a dog and the robot he created is shown in expressive, almost wordless, graphic panels. (8–11)

A Song for Harlem: Scraps of Time 1928
by Patricia C. McKissack,
ill. by Gordon C. James
(Viking, $14.99) 978-0-670-06209-6
As part of a young writers workshop, Lilly Belle comes to Harlem where she experiences the Harlem Renaissance. (8–11)

Summerhouse Time
by Eileen Spinelli, ill. by Joanne Lew-Vriethoff
(Knopf, $12.99) 978-0-375-84061-6
Eleven-year-old Sophie shares joys and woes when she joins her extended family for their annual stay at the beach house. (9–12)

Why? The War Years
written and ill. by Tomie dePaola
(Putnam, $14.99) 978-0-399-24692-0
The war surrounds an eight-year-old in 1942. (8–10)

HUMOR

The Fabled Fourth Graders of Aesop Elementary School
by Candace Fleming
(S&W, $15.99) 978-0-375-83672-5
Skulls on the teacher's desk, nose rings for class pictures and a boy named Ashley inspire unexpected morals. (8–10)

★No Talking
by Andrew Clements, ill. by Mark Elliot
(S&S, $15.99) 978-1-4169-0983-5
Dave learns about Mahatma Gandhi, and a whole new world of communication (and competition with the girls)opens to him. (8–11)

PAST

★Ain't Nobody a Stranger to Me
by Ann Grifalconi, ill. by Jerry Pinkney
(Jump At The Sun, $16.99) 978-0-7868-1857-0
Gran'pa shares memories of his daring escape from slavery to freedom on the Underground Railroad. Watercolors of today contrast with sepia tones of hardship. (9–11)

Attack of the Turtle
by Drew Carlson
(Eerdmans, $16) 978-0-8028-5308-0
A boy overcomes his fears and helps fight the British with a top-secret new weapon—the first submarine. (9–11)

Billy Creekmore
by Tracey Porter
(HarperCollins, $17.89) 978-0-06-077571-1
In 1905, a storytelling ten-year-old escapes from a cruel orphanage and finds many challenging adventures. (9–12)

Blown Away!
by Joan Hiatt Harlow
(McElderry, $15.99) 978-1-4169-0781-7
During the devastating 1935 hurricane in the Florida keys, thirteen-year-old Jake learns about life and survival. (9–12)

The Cemetery Keepers Of Gettysburg
by Linda Oatman High,
ill. by Laura Francesca Filippucci
(Walker, $16.95) 978-0-8027-8094-2
With the father away, a family struggles to bury the dead from the Battle of Gettysburg. Watercolors heightened with brown ink. (8–12)

★Chase
by Jessie Haas
(Greenwillow, $16.99) 978-0-06-112850-9
Witnessing a murder by an Irish secret society member, Phin flees, pursued by a detective and his horse that tracks like a bloodhound. (9–14)

The Day The Stones Walked: A Tale of Easter Island
by T.A. Barron, ill. by William Low
(Philomel, $16.99) 978-0-399-24263-2
When a tsunami threatens his island, Pico understands about the giant stone faces. Expressive computer-generated illustrations. (8–11)

Elijah of Buxton
by Christopher Paul Curtis
(Scholastic, $16.99) 978-0-439-02344-3
Born in freedom in Buxton, Canada in 1860, eleven-year old Elijah goes to school, helps on the farm until... he is thrust into the terrible life that might have been. (11–13)

The Ever-After Bird
by Ann Rinaldi
(Harcourt, $17) 978-0-15-202620-2
When Cece accompanies her ornithologist uncle on a search through 1851 Georgia for the scarlet ibis, she learns there is a secret mission. (10–13)

A Friendship For Today
by Patricia C. McKissack
(Scholastic, $16.99) 978-0-439-66098-3
When desegregation comes to Missouri, sixth-grader Rosemary is the only African American in her class. (9–12)

★Henry's Freedom Box: A True Story From The Underground Railroad
by Ellen Levine, ill. by Kadir Nelson
(Scholastic, $16.99) 978-0-439-77733-9
An enslaved man escapes to the north in an unusual way. Based on a true story. Expressive illustrations. (8–12)

★Hitler's Canary
by Sandi Toksvig
(Roaring Brook, $16.95) 978-1-59643-247-5
During World War II a Danish theatrical family must face Nazi occupation and decide how to fight the persecution of the Jews. (9–14)

Iron Thunder: The Battle Between the Monitor & the Merrimac
by Avi, ill. by C.B. Mordan
(Hyperion, $15.99) 978-1-4231-0446-9
A thirteen-year-old needing a job unexpectedly finds himself at the center of a famous naval battle. (10–12)

The Lacemaker And The Princess
by Kimberly Brubaker Bradley
(McElderry, $16.99) 978-1-4169-1920-9
In the last days of the French monarchy, two young girls have an unusual friendship in Versailles (9–12)

Letters From The Corrugated Castle: A Novel of Gold Rush California, 1850-1852
by Joan W. Blos
(Atheneum, $17.99) 978-0-689-87077-4
Thirteen-year-old Eudora meets the mother who lost her and learns compassion for poor Mexican children. (9–12)

Magic in the Margins: A Medieval Tale of Bookmaking
by W. Nikola-Lisa, ill. by Bonnie Christensen
(HMC, $17) 978-0-618-49642-6
Simon, apprentice scribe to the monks, learns the meaning of imagination as he aspires to illuminate a manuscript. Ink and tempera illuminations. (8–11)

★On the Wings of Heroes
by Richard Peck
(Dial, $16.99) 978-0-8037-3081-6
In a small Illinois town during World War II, Davy describes the home front chores and poignancy of an older brother going off to war. (9–12)

Pappy's Handkerchief
by Devin Scillian, ill. by Chris Ellison
(Sleeping Bear, $17.95) 978-1-58536-316-2
In 1889, Moses and his family leave Baltimore to join the many other African-American families making a stake in the Oklahoma land run. Painterly illustrations. (8–11)

Rex Zero and the End of the World
by Tim Wynne-Jones
(FSG, $16) 978-0-374-33467-3
Rex Zero, on the trail of an escaped panther who may be hiding out in Ottawa's Adams Park, makes friends during the hunt. (9–12)

The Silver Cup
by Constance Leeds
(Viking, $16.99) 978-0-670-06157-0
In the eleventh century, fifteen-year-old Anna insists on harboring a Jewish girl in her small German Catholic village. (10–14)

Sitting Bull Remembers
by Ann Turner, paintings by Wendell Minor
(HarperCollins, $17.89) 978-0-06-051400-6
Lyrical text and expressive, realistic illustrations reflect the life of the great Sioux leader. (8–10)

Someone Named Eva
by Joan M. Wolf
(Clarion, $16) 978-0-618-53579-8
Seized in Lidice in 1940, eleven-year-old Milada struggles to maintain her Czech identity throughout the Nazi occupation. (9–12)

Stone Age Boy
written and ill. by Satoshi Kitamura
(Candlewick, $15.99) 978-0-7636-3474-2
Lively detailed illustrations help tell the story about life in the Stone Age. (8–10)

The Story of Jonas
by Maurine F. Dahlberg
(FSG, $16) 978-0-374-37264-4
A young slave's trip to the Kansas gold fields with a brutal young master becomes a journey toward freedom. (9–12)

The Voyageur's Paddle
by Kathy-jo Wargin, ill. by David Geister
(Sleeping Bear, $17.95) 978-1-58536-007-9
Living in the Great lakes region, Jacques waits patiently to help paddle to the trading post just as his father does. Soft, realistic illustrations. (8–11)

War Horse
by Michael Morpurgo
(Scholastic, $16.99) 978-0-439-79663-7
Facing the terrors of a World War I battlefront, a former farm horse searches constantly for the gentle boy who was his master. Powerful and moving. (9–12)

Way Down Deep
by Ruth White
(FSG, $16) 978-0-374-38251-3
Why is the red-haired toddler on the courthouse steps? And how does she manage to change the lives of so many? (9–12)

Who's Saying What In Jamestown, Thomas Savage?
by Jean Fritz, ill. by Sally Wern Comport
(Putnam, $18.99) 978-0-399-24644-9
The life of a thirteen-year-old boy and the beginning of the English colony at Jamestown are explored in a lively narrative. (9–12)

NEW BEGINNINGS: LIFE IN A NEW LAND

FIVE TO NINE

At Home in a New Land (I Can Read Book Series: Level 3)

by Joan Sandin
(HarperCollins, 2007, $15.99)
978-0-06-058077-3

When Carl Erik came to Minnesota from Sweden with his family, he encountered many challenges as a new immigrant. Realistic illustrations.

Candy Shop

by Jan Wahl, ill. by Nicole Wong
(Charlesbridge, 2005, $6.95)
978-1-57091-668-7

When a boy and his aunt find that a bigot has written hurtful words on the sidewalk just outside the candy shop owned by "Miz Chu," a new immigrant from Taiwan, they set out to comfort her.

The Color of Home

by Mary Hoffman, ill. by Karin Littlewood
(Penguin, 2002, $17.99) 978-0-8037-2841-7

Hassan, newly-arrived in the United States and feeling homesick, paints a picture at school that shows his old home in Somalia as well as the reason his family had to leave.

I Hate English!

by Ellen Levine, illus. by Steve Bjorkman

NINE TO TWELVE

Blood on the River: James Town 1607

by Elisa Lynn Carbone
(Penguin, 2007, $6.99) 978-0-1424-0932-9

Twelve-year-old Samuel travels with Captain John Smith into James Town and learns to survive the hardships of the wilderness.

Esperanza Rising

by Pam Muñoz Ryan
(Scholastic, 2002, $6.99) 978-0-439-12042-5

When her father's death ends her privileged childhood in Mexico, Esperanza must adjust to life in a California migrant camp.

Eclipse

by Andrea Cheng
(Front Street, 2006, $16.95)
978-1-932425-21-5

Peti struggles with the intrusion of recently emigrated relatives and his grandfather's entrapment behind the Iron Curtain in 1952 Hungary.

In the Year of the Boar and Jackie Robinson

by Bette Bao Lord, ill. by Marc Simont
(HarperCollins, 1986, $5.99)
978-0-06-440175-3

A ten-year-old Chinese girl adjusts to life in Brooklyn in 1947.

The Witch of Blackbird Pond

by Elizabeth George Speare
(Random, 1972, $6.99) 978-0-440-49596-3

A young girl travels from a liberal home in Barbados to a relatively conservative one in 1867 Connecticut.

TWELVE & UP

The Arrival

by Shaun Tan
(Scholastic, 2007, $19.99)
978-0-439-89529-3

A man seeks a new life for his family in a strange new world in a haunting, wordless story. Extraordinary, realistic, sepia illustrations.

Ask Me No Questions

by Marina Budhos
(S&S, 2007, $8.99) 978-1-416-94920-6

Two Bangladeshi sisters succeed in high school when their father, an illegal alien, is taken into custody.

Does My Head Look Big in This?

by Randa Abdel-Fattah
(Scholastic, Inc., 2007, $16.99)
978-0-439-91947-0

An eleventh-grade Australian-Palestinian girl struggles with her decision to wear the hijab (Muslim head scarf).

by Esther Rudomin Hautzig
(HarperCollins 1995, $5.99)
978-0-06-440577-5
The author's memoir describes when she and her Jewish family were arrested in Poland by the Russians during World War II and exiled to Siberia.

Flight to Freedom

By Ana Veciana-Suarez
(Orchard, $16.95) 0-439-38199-1
Thirteen-year-old Yara writes in her diary about her family's life in Cuba and their exile to America in the 1960s.

My Name is Aram: A Joyful Portrait of American Immigrant Life

By William Saroyan
(Laurel, $24.99) 978-0-0440-36205-0
Born in California into a family of immigrant Americans, Aram learns the power of dreams.

Nory Ryan's Song

by Patricia Reilly Giff
(Delacorte, 2002, P$6.50)
978-0-385-32141-4
When the potato famine strikes Ireland in 1845, twelve-year-old Nory helps her family and neighbors survive.

(Random, 2007, $6.50) 978-0-553-49416-7
In 1892 a nine-year-old stows away from Napoli and survives alone on the streets of New York.

Letters from the Corrugated Castle: A Novel of Gold Rush California, 1850-1852

by Joan W. Blos
(S&S, 2007, $17.99) 978-0-6898-7077-4
Thirteen-year-old Eudora meets the mother who lost her and learns compassion for poor Mexican children.

Lowji Discovers America

by Candace Fleming
(S&S, 2005, $15.95) 978-0-6898-6299-1
Moving to a new country is hard, but with a little bit of pluck anything is possible.

Project Mulberry

by Linda Sue Park
(Random, 2007, $6.50) 978-0-440-42163-4
Korean-American Julia worries about ethnic misunderstandings and other complex issues as she and her friend Patrick work on a silkworm project for the state fair.

The Trouble Begins

by Linda Himelblau
(Random, 2005, $14.95) 978-0-385-73273-4
Du not only has to adjust to life in the U.S., but also to life with his family, since he and his grandmother had to stay in the Philippines when the rest of the family escaped from Vietnam.

---

adjust to school and learn the alien sounds of English.

Marianthe's Story: Painted Words and Marianthe's Story: Spoken Memories

by Aliki
(Greenwillow, 1998, $16.99)
978-0-68-815661-9
Presented as two stories in one, a young girl paints to adjust to a new language and a new school.

My Name Is Yoon

by Helen Recorvits, ill. Gabi Swiatkowska
(Frances Foster, 2003, $16.00)
978-0-374-35114-4
A young Korean girl comes to accept her new life in America through words: cat, bird, cupcake and finally her own name.

When This World Was New

by D. H. Figueredo,
ill. by Enrique O. Sanchez
(Lee & Low, 1999, $6.95)
978-1-58430-173-8
When his father leads him on a magical trip of discovery through new-fallen snow, a young boy who emigrated from his warm island home overcomes fears about living in New York.

★Wind Rider

by Susan Williams
(HarperCollins, $16.99) '06 978-0-06-087236-6
A girl's domestication of a horse in prehistoric times deeply affects those around her. (9–12)

SCIENCE FICTION

The Rules Of The Universe By Austin W. Hale

by Robin Vaupel
(Holiday House, $16.95) 978-0-8234-1811-4
When Austin's Nobel Prize-winning grandfather comes to live with the Hales in his last illness, the thirteen-year old faces new challenges in science and life. (10–12)

★The True Meaning of Smekday

written and ill. by Adam Rex
(Hyperion, $16.99) 978-0-7868-4900-0
Fully illustrated, this funny tale of alien invasion depicts the unusual friendship of Gratuity Tucci and the Boov, J.Lo. (9–12)

SPORTS

Champions on the Bench: The Cannon Street YMCA All-Stars

by Carole Boston Weatherford,
ill. by Leonard Jenkins
(Dial, $16.99) 978-0-8037-2987-2
A young boy, full of dreams and hopes, faces the discrimination of 1955 against his African-American Little League team. Impressionistic acrylic and spray paint illustrations. (8–10)

Mack McGinn's Big Win

by Coleen Murtagh Paratore
(S&S, $15.99) 978-1-4169-1613-0
In Mack's struggle to prove he is best at something, he inadvertently shows his family what matters to him most. (9–12)

Summer Ball

by Mike Lupica
(Philomel, $17.99) 978-0-399-24487-2
Thirteen-year-old Danny, a champion (but short) basketball player, goes to a prestigious camp and finds that he makes both friends and enemies. (10–13)

TODAY

The Bee Tree

by Stephen Buchmann, and Diana Cohn,
ill. by Paul Mirocha
(Cinco Puntos Press, $17.95)
978-0-938317-98-2
As a rite of passage, a young boy from a honey-hunting clan in Malaysia must climb the tallest rainforest tree in the dark of night. (8–11)

★A Crooked Kind of Perfect

by Linda Urban
(Harcourt, $16) 978-0-15-206007-7
Zoe wants a piano and gets a secondhand organ. Her performance at a competition, amidst difficult family circumstances helps her achieve her dreams. (10–13)

How to Steal a Dog

by Barbara O'Connor
(FSG, $16) 978-0-374-33497-0
Georgina, who lives in an old car, devises a disastrous plan to improve her family's fortunes. (9–12)

The Man with the Red Bag

by Eve Bunting
(Joanna Cotler Books, $16.89)
978-0-06-081835-7
Nine months after 9/11, twelve-year-old Kevin is touring Western landmarks with his grandmother. Can the odd looking passenger be trusted? (9–12)

Peiling and the Chicken-Fried Christmas

by Pauline Chen
(Bloomsbury, $15.95) 978-1-59990-122-0
Fifth grader Peiling Wang wants to celebrate Christmas like her American friends, but her traditional Taiwanese-American father has other ideas. (8–11)

The Qwikpick Adventure Society

by Sam Riddleburger
(Dial, $16.99) 978-0-8037-3178-3
An unlikely trio of friends spends Christmas
in a very unlikely way. (10–12)

★Reaching For Sun

by Tracie Vaughn Zimmer
(Bloomsbury, $14.95) 978-1-59990-037-7
Thirteen-year-old Josie shares her year of
growth as she deals with cerebral palsy and
lessons from the family garden. In free verse.
(10–14)

★Rickshaw Girl

by Mitali Perkins, ill. by Jamie Hogan
(Charlesbridge, $13.95) 978-1-58089-308-4
Naima, a resourceful Bangladeshi girl, steps
out of traditional women's occupations to
help her family while using her artistic talents.
(8–10)

TWELVE & UP

ADVENTURE AND MYSTERY

Edenville Owls
by Robert B. Parker
(Philomel, $17.99) 978-0-399-24656-2
Just after World War II, fourteen-year-old
Bobby enlists his friends' help to solve his
teacher's problem and his own dilemmas.
(11–14)

Eye of the Crow
by Shane Peacock
(Tundra, $19.95) 978-0-88776-850-7
At age thirteen Sherlock Holmes already
reveals his brilliant mind and psychological
trappings. Details of London life in the 1860s.
(12–14)

Falling From Grace
by Jane Godwin
(Holiday House, $16.95) 978-0-8234-2105-3
A girl's disappearance during a terrible night
storm off the coast of Australia is described
from differing points of view. (11–14)

📖 Manga Shakespeare: Hamlet
ill. by Emma Vieceli
(Amulet, P$9.95) 978-0-8109-9324-2
Set in the future, Shakespeare's contemplative
hero deals with murder, intrigue and danger.
(12–14)

FANTASY

★The Arrival
written and ill. by Shaun Tan
(Arthur A. Levine, $19.99) 978-0-439-89529-3
The haunting wordless story describes a man
seeking a new life for his family in a strange new
world. Extraordinary, realistic sepia illustrations.
(11–14)

★Book of a Thousand Days
by Shannon Hale
(Bloomsbury, $17.95) 978-1-59990-051-3
Imprisoned in a tower with her young mis-
tress, fifteen-year-old Dashti uses her gifts of
healing, courage and insights to survive.
(11–14)

Raymond Briggs 2005

★Faeries Of Dreamdark: Blackbringer
by Laini Taylor
(Putnam, $17.99) 978-0-399-24630-2
Magpie Windwitch sets off to capture a new
devil but must battle evil far worse than she
has ever known. (11–15)

The Hollow People
by Brian Keaney
(Knopf, $16.99) 978-0-375-84332-7
An authoritarian government headed by evil
Dr. Sigmundus controls its population with
drugs, but a stalwart band resists by exploring
reality's limits. (11–14)

The Land Of The Silver Apples
by Nancy Farmer
(Atheneum, $18.99) 978-1-4169-0735-0
Amidst the conflicting beliefs of eighth-centu-
ry Britain, a quest leads Jack to Elfland and
the truth about his sister Lucy. (11–14)

★The New Policeman
by Kate Thompson
(Greenwillow, $16.99) 978-0-06-117427-8
While journeying in another world to find
more time for his mother, J. J. discovers a family secret. (11–14)

The Night Tourist
by Katherine Marsh
(Hyperion, $17.99) 978-1-4231-0689-0
In this suspenseful retelling of the Orpheus legend, a lonely prodigy, Jack Perdu, has an adventure in Manhattan's underground. (11–14)

Powers
by Ursula K. Le Guin
(Harcourt, $17) 978-0-15-205770-1
After his sister is killed, the slave Gavir leaves his master's house and attempts to learn about himself and his identity. (12–14)

The Princess and the Hound
by Mette Ivie Harrison
(HarperCollins, $18.89) 978-0-06-113188-2
Prince George has "animal magic" in a kingdom that bars it. He marries a princess of a rival kingdom, whom he met first as a hound. (12–14)

Skin Hunger
by Kathleen Duey
(Atheneum, $17.99) 978-0-689-84093-7
The lives of Sadima and Hahp are divided by centuries but united in their search for true magic. (12–16)

Waves
by Sharon Dogar
(Chicken House, $16.99) 978-0-439-87180-8
Fifteen-year-old Hal unravels the mystery of his sister's accident through their supernatural connection. (12–15)

Wildwood Dancing
by Juliet Marillier
(Knopf, $16.99) 978-0-375-83364-9
Five daring sisters, an unusual frog and a monthly portal into a mysterious parallel world fill this tale of heroines. (12–14)

GROWING UP

★The Absolutely True Diary of a Part-Time Indian
by Sherman Alexie, ill. by Ellen Forney
(Little, $16.99) 978-0-316-01368-0
Junior tackles basketball, his ex-best friend, poverty, puberty and hope after leaving a reservation to attend an all-white school. (12–16) M

★Beauty Shop For Rent... fully equipped, inquire within
by Laura Bowers
(Harcourt, $17) 978-0-15-205764-0
Fourteen-year-old Abbey establishes a support system and learns to trust people in this quirky, humorous story. (12–15)

The Breakup Bible
by Melissa Kantor
(Hyperion, $15.99) 978-0-7868-0962-2
Learning what matters helps high-school junior Jen grow through the turmoil of a romantic breakup. (12–14)

The Corps Of The Bare-Boned Plane
by Polly Horvath
(FSG, $17) 978-0-374-31553-5
After their parents' death, teenage cousins are sent to live with their eccentric uncle on an isolated island to deal with their grief. (12–15)

Diamonds in the Shadow
by Caroline B. Cooney
(Delacorte, $15.99) 978-0-385-73261-1
A generous, but initially clueless, American family host African refugees with a horrific past and a sinister, dangerous secret. (12–15)

★Home of the Brave
by Katherine Applegate
(Feiwel, $16.95) 978-0-312-36765-7
Kek, a ten-year-old Sudanese refugee from the horrors of war, finds friendship, hope and the possibility of a new life in Minnesota. (10–14)

Kissing The Bee
by Kathe Koja
(FSG, $16) 978-0-374-39938-2
Dana falls in love with her best friend Avra's boyfriend, Emil. (12–14)

★Memoirs of a Teenage Amnesiac
by Gabrielle Zevin
(FSG, $17) 978-0-374-34946-2
When head trauma blocks out four years of Naomi's life, she gains a new perspective on complicated personal relationships. (12–14)

The Mysterious Edge of the Heroic World
by E.L. Konigsburg
(Atheneum, $16.99) 978-1-4169-4972-5
As he gets to know his eccentric neighbor, eleven-year-old Amadeo has a hunch that his dream of making an important discovery may be fulfilled. (11–13)

★The Off Season
by Catherine Gilbert Murdock
(HMC, $16) 978-0-618-68695-7
All D.J.'s resources are called upon when his football star brother, Win, is paralyzed by an injury. (12–14)

★The Poison Apples
by Lily Archer
(Feiwel, $16.95) 978-0-312-36762-6
Boarding school buddies Alice, Reena and Molly's plots of revenge against their evil step-mothers take some unexpected twists and turns. (11–14)

The Secret Life Of Sparrow Delaney
by Suzanne Harper
(Greenwillow, $17.89) 978-0-06-113159-2
Communicating with spirits is the family business, but Sparrow hides her extraordinary powers until a persistent ghost persuades her to solve a mystery. (12–14)

Shining On: 11 Star Authors' Illuminating Stories
forward by Lois Lowry
(Delacorte, $P8.99) 978-0-385-73472-1
Well-known authors explore the trials and tribulations of growing up. (12–16)

The Silenced
by James DeVita
(HarperCollins, $18.89) 978-0-06-078464-5
Marina struggles bravely and creatively against the grim totalitarian system in which she lives. (12–14)

Someday This Pain Will Be Useful To You
by Peter Cameron
(FSG, $16) 978-0-374-30989-3
James is eighteen, doesn't fit anywhere, doesn't like people, fears going to college and acts out. (12–15)

Strange Relations
by Sonia Levitin
(Knopf, $15.99) 978-0-375-83751-7
The culture shock of her summer with Chasidic relatives in Hawaii leads to growth and understanding for Marne. (12–15)

★Strays
by Ron Koertge
(Candlewick, $16.99) 978-0-7636-2705-8
Sixteen-year-old Ted communicates better with animals than with humans, as he endures his life in a foster home. (12–14)

★Undercover
by Beth Kephart
(HarperCollins, $17.89) 978-0-06-123894-9
By way of a female Cyrano character, Elisa immerses herself in poetry and explores her identity. (12–14)

The Very Ordered Existence of Merilee Marvelous
by Suzanne Crowley
(Greenwillow, $16.99) 978-0-06-123197-1
The arrival of strangers in town makes it impossible for Merilee to stick to her schedule. (10–14)

★What My Girlfriend Doesn't Know
by Sonya Sones
(S&S, $16.99) 978-0-689-87602-8
Fourteen-year-old Robin and his girlfriend, Sophie, confront the class bullies as well as the changes in their budding relationship. A free-verse novel. (12–15)

★The Whole Sky Full of Stars
by René Saldaña, Jr.
(Wendy Lamb, $15.99) 978-0-385-73053-2
After his father dies, Barry's friendships and goals are questioned when he considers a shady boxing gamble. (12–16)

Zen and the Art of Faking It

by Jordan Sonnenblick
(Scholastic, $16.99) 978-0-439-83707-1
A new boy tries to fit into school by acting
like a Zen master. Does his practice trip him
up or enlighten him? (12–14)

PAST

★Archie's War: My Scrapbook of the First World War, 1914-1918

written and ill. by Marcia Williams
(Candlewick, $17.99) 978-0-7636-3532-9
The daily life of a London boy during World
War II is vivid and poignantly detailed in this
graphic-style scrapbook format. (11–14)

★Bone by Bone by Bone

by Tony Johnston
(Roaring Brook, $17.95) 978-1-59643-113-3
In 1940s Tennessee, nine-year-old David finds
a best friend and learns the deep hurt and
consequences of hate and racism. (12–14)

Born For Adventure

by Kathleen Karr
(Cavendish, $16.99) 978-0-7614-5348-2
Tom, a chemist's assistant, talks his way into
accompanying Henry Morton Stanley on an
expedition into the African jungle of 1887.
(11–14)

★Cracker!: The Best Dog in Vietnam

by Cynthia Kadohata
(Atheneum, $16.99) 978-1-4169-0637-7
During the Vietnamese War, a German shep-
herd and his handler team up to search for
the enemy, bombs and traps. Told from the
dog's point of view. (12–14)

Duchessina: A Novel Of Catherine de' Medici

by Carolyn Meyer
(Harcourt, $17) 978-0-15-205588-2
With Rome and Florence vying for control of
sixteenth century Italy, Catherine survives jeal-
ousy, greed and disease to become the consort
of France's Henry II. (12–14)

Enter Three Witches

by Caroline B. Cooney
(Scholastic, $16.99) 978-0-439-71156-2
Fourteen-year-old Lady Mary is caught up in
the events surrounding her treacherous
Scottish relatives, Lord and Lady MacBeth.
(12–14)

★Factory Girl

by Barbara Greenwood
(Kids Can, P$12.95) 978-1-55337-648-4
In 1905, a twelve-year-old girl works 11 hours
a day in a garment factory to keep her family
from starving. (11–14)

Good Masters! Sweet Ladies!: Voices From A Medieval Village

by Laura Amy Schlitz, ill. by Robert Byrd
(Candlewick, $19.99) 978-0-7636-1578-9
The residents of a medieval English village
present their lives in poetic monologues
enriched by period pen-and-ink illustrations.
(11–14)

Greetings From Planet Earth

by Barbara Kerley
(Scholastic, $16.99) 978-0-439-80203-1
Twelve-year-old Theo's father has not yet
returned from Vietnam in 1977. Though no
one will talk about him, Theo attempts to
solve the mystery. (11–13)

Harlem Summer

by Walter Dean Myers
(Scholastic, $16.99) 978-0-439-36843-8
Sixteen-year-old Mark encounters outstanding
people in the arts and noted gangland figures
while he seeks to play his "sax" in 1925
Harlem. (11–14)

Hush: An Irish Princess' Tale

by Donna Jo Napoli
(Atheneum, $16.99) 978-0-689-86176-5
A haunting retelling of an enslaved celtic
princess's hardships and her discovery of
power and hope amidst powerlessness.
(12–14) M

★Keeping Corner

by Kashmira Sheth
(Hyperion, $15.99) 978-0-7868-3859-2
In Gandhi's India, a twelve-year-old girl is
stripped of her colorful saris and light-hearted
ways as she mourns. (12–14)

★Letters from a Slave Boy: The Story of Joseph Jacobs
by Mary E. Lyons
(Atheneum, $15.99) 978-0-689-87867-1
Joseph's escape from slavery in North Carolina includes life aboard a New Bedford whaler and gold prospecting in California. Carefully researched. (12–14)

The Miner's Daughter
by Gretchen Moran Laskas
(S&S, $15.99) 978-1-4169-1262-0
A gritty survivor, Willa longs for a life beyond what depression-ridden West Virginia is able to offer. (12–14)

Pure Spring
by Brian Doyle
(Groundwood, $16.95) 978-0-88899-774-6
When Martin lies about his age to get a job, he leaves himself open to blackmail and risks losing his girlfriend. (11–14)

Raleigh's Page
by Alan Armstrong, ill. by Tim Jessell
(Random, $16.99) 978-0-375-83319-9
In the late 1500s, an eleven-year-old sets sail for the wilderness of Virginia where he experiences hardship, adventure and harsh treatment of Native Americans. (11–14)

★Revolution Is Not a Dinner Party
by Ying Chang Compestine
(Henry Holt, $16.95) 978-0-8050-8207-4
Nine-year-old Ling watches her world crumble as the 1972 Cultural Revolution in China labels her family members as enemies of the state. (12–14)

★Song of the Sparrow
by Lisa Ann Sandell
(Scholastic, $16.99) 978-0-439-91848-0
A prose-poem based on the Tales of King Arthur and his Knights of the Round Table told from a feminist point of view. (12–14)

A Tale of Gold
by Thelma Hatch Wyss
(McElderry, $16.99) 978-1-4169-4212-2
When gold is discovered in the Yukon, a fourteen-year-old orphan joins the stampede north, picking up unlikely partners along the way. (12–14)

Tough Times
by Milton Meltzer
(Clarion, $16) 978-0-618-87445-3
Fifteen-year-old Joey braves the hard times of the Great Depression and the Bonus March of 1932 until it becomes almost unbearable. (12–14)

The Traitors' Gate
by Avi
(Atheneum, $17.99) 978-0-689-85335-7
In 1849 London, fourteen-year-old John struggles to solve the mystery of a scheme which lands his father in debtor's prison. (11–14)

Uprising
by Margaret Peterson Haddix
(S&S, $16.99) 978-1-4169-1171-5
Three young women—two poor, one privileged—are brought together through the early twentieth century labor movement and then devastated by the Triangle Shirtwaist fire. (12–14)

When I Crossed No-Bob
by Margaret McMullan
(HMC, $16) 978-0-618-71715-6
In rural Mississippi during Reconstruction, twelve-year-old Addy faces the challenges of poverty and violent racism with integrity and courage. (11–13)

Raymond Briggs 2005

TWELVE & UP

SCIENCE FICTION

The Book of Time: Volume I
by Guillaume Prévost,
trans. by William Rodarmor
(Arthur A. Levine, $16.99) 978-0-439-88375-7
In search of his missing father, Sam finds a path that takes him back in time to old Ireland, ancient Egypt and other exciting places by following clues. (11–14)

Extras
by Scott Westerfeld
(Simon Pulse, $16.99) 978-1-4169-5117-9
In this exciting story, set in a parallel universe, fifteen-year-old Aya meets the sly girls and life becomes more dangerous. (12–14)

★First Light
by Rebecca Stead
(Wendy Lamb, $15.99) 978-0-375-84017-3
Two protagonists from two worlds meet as Peter joins his scientist parents to research global warming. (12–14)

Hungry
by Alethea Eason
(Eos, $16.89) 978-0-06-082555-3
Life in middle school can be very challenging—especially if you're an alien and need to choose between making friends and eating them. (11–13)

★Unwind
by Neal Shusterman
(S&S, $16.99) 978-1-4169-1204-0
Connor, Lev and Risa struggle to survive in a world where teenagers can be "unwound" to have their body parts salvaged. (12–14) M

SPORTS

Cover-Up: Mystery at the Super Bowl
by John Feinstein
(Knopf, $16.99) 978-0-375-84247-4
Steve and Susan Carol, intrepid fourteen-year-old sports reporters, cover the big football game—and stumble on a doping cover-up. (12–14)

Toby Wheeler: Eighth-Grade Benchwarmer
by Thatcher Heldring
(Delacorte, $14.99) 978-0-385-73390-8
A tough coach enables Toby to sharpen his basketball skills and become a valuable team player. (11–14)

TODAY

★Beige
by Cecil Castellucci
(Candlewick, $16.99) 978-0-7636-3066-9
When fourteen-year-old Katy spends the summer in Los Angeles getting to know her "punk rock" father, she also gets to know herself. (12–14)

Does My Head Look Big In This?
by Randa Abdel-Fattah
(Orchard, $16.99) 978-0-439-91947-0
An eleventh-grade Australian-Palestinian girl struggles with her decision to wear the hijab (Muslim head scarf). (12–14)

Evolution, Me, & Other Freaks of Nature
by Robin Brande
(Knopf, $15.99) 978-0-375-84349-5
Mena's fundamentalist upbringing clashes with her growing sense of other possibilities, such as compassion, evolution and a boyfriend. (11–13)

Finding Stinko
by Michael de Guzman
(FSG, $16) 978-0-374-32305-9
Twelve-year-old Newboy, mute for three years, needs a new life. Who would think a ventriloquist's dummy would be such a lucky find? (12–14)

Harmless
by Dana Reinhardt
(Wendy Lamb, $15.99) 978-0-385-74699-1
Caught in a lie by their parents, three fifteen-year-old friends fabricate an elaborate, outrageous excuse—with devastating results. (12–14) M

Kat Got Your Tongue
by Lee Weatherly
(David Fickling Books, $15.99)
978-0-385-75117-9
Kat struggles to deal with profound amnesia
and the mystery of what really caused it.
(11–14)

★Lemonade Mouth
by Mark Peter Hughes
(Delacorte, $15.99) 978-0-385-73392-2
An unlikely quintet of mostly socially margin-
al high school freshmen forms a band, creating amazing music—and much more. (12–14)

Parrotfish
by Ellen Wittlinger
(S&S, $16.99) 978-1-4169-1622-2
A transgendered youth connects with a geek,
a teacher and his family as he embraces life as
a male. (12–14)

Payback
by James Heneghan
(Groundwood, $17.95) 978-0-88899-701-2
Charley, thirteen-years-old, new and defense-
less in Vancouver, fails to stop Benny's bully-
ing which ends in tragedy. (12–14) M

Quaking
by Kathryn Erskine
(Philomel, $16.99) 978-0-399-24774-3
Living with Quakers, fourteen-year-old Matt
learns to stand up for her beliefs and face her
fear of bullies. (12–14) M

Raymond Briggs 2005

Saints Of Augustine
by P.E. Ryan
(Harper Teen, $17.89) 978-0-06-085811-7
Charlie and Sam are in crisis. Charlie must
adjust to his mother's death and Sam to the
knowledge he's gay. (11–14)

★Shark Girl
by Kelly Bingham
(Candlewick, $16.99) 978-0-7636-3207-6
Victim of a shark attack, fifteen-year-old Jane
has to face high school without her right arm.
(12–14)

Tall Tales
by Karen Day
(Wendy Lamb, $15.99) 978-0-375-83773-9
When Meg moves again to a new town, her
lies about her father's drinking threaten an
important new friendship. (11–13)

Special Interests

ACTIVITIES

Alter This!: Radical Ideas for Transforming Books into Art
by Alena Hennessy
(Lark Books, $14.95) 978-1-57990-948-2
Innovative suggestions include helpful tips and techniques. Amply illustrated. (9–12)

• ECOCRAFTS

Creative Costumes
by Dawn Brend

Gorgeous Gifts
by Rebecca Craig

Jazzy Jewelry
by Dawn Brend
(Kingfisher, P$7.95) 978-0-7534-5968-3, 978-0-7534-5967-6, 978-0-7534-5969-0
Creative uses for items usually not recycled. (6–9)

★How Many: Spectacular Paper Sculptures
by Ron van der Meer
(Random, $24.99) 978-0-375-84226-9
Exquisite designs invite discovery of different shapes and colors through an interactive format. (6–9)

I Love To Draw Cartoons!
written and ill. by Jennifer Lipsey
(Lark Books, $9.95) 978-1-57990-819-5
Easy-to-follow sequences of shapes show young children how to draw people and animals in cartoon style. (8–10)

I Spy Colors in Art
devised and selected by Lucy Micklethwait
(Greenwillow, $19.99) 978-0-06-134837-2
A look at ancient and modern paintings while playing the traditional I Spy game fosters an appreciation of art in young children. (3–6)

Raymond Briggs 2005

If You Were a Palindrome
by Michael Dahl, ill. by Sara Gray
(Picture Window, $25.26) 978-1-4048-3162-9
The magical words that work backwards as well as forwards are illustrated with bold examples and vibrant acrylic artwork. (4–7)

Maze Ways A To Z
written and ill. by Roxie Munro
(Sterling, $12.95) 978-1-4027-3774-9
These twenty-six adventures with 700 hidden objects to discover have mind-bending illustrations. (8–11)

Mother Goose Unplucked: Crazy Comics, Zany Activities, Nutty Facts & Other Twisted Takes on Childhood Favorites
by Helaine Becker, ill. by Claudia Dávila
(Maple Tree Press, $10.95) 978-1-897066-84-3
Many enjoyable activities based on Mother Goose stories, including twisted tales, are great for travel and rainy days. Colorful illustrations. (8–12)

Ralph Masiello's Dragon Drawing Book: Become An Artist Step-By-Step
written and ill. by Ralph Masiello
(Charlesbridge, $16.95) 978-1-57091-531-4
Follow the clear steps for drawing famous mythical dragons. (9–11)

37

...ACTIVITIES

Ribbit!:
Flip and See Who Froggy Can Be
written and ill. by Bender & Bender
(HarperCollins, $16.99) 978-0-06-113820-1
With a flip of a strip, a frog's character is
transformed thousands of times. Bright colors
on black backgrounds. (4–6)

ARTS

★600 Black Spots:
A Pop-Up Book for
Children of All Ages
by David A. Carter,
paper engineering by David A. Carter
(Little Simon, $19.99) 978-1-4169-4092-0
Museum-quality, colorful and intricate paper-
engineered sculptures are unified by their
inclusion of black dots throughout. (6–15)

★Artist to Artist:
23 Major Illustrators Talk
to Children About Their Art
edited by Patricia Lee Gauch et al.
(Philomel, $30) 978-0-399-24600-5
Favorite artists speak to children about illus-
trating. Includes pictures from all phases of
their lives. (7–12)

★Ballerina Dreams
by Lauren Thompson, photos by James Estrin
(Feiwel, $16.95) 978-0-312-37029-9
Through hard work, an inspiring teacher, and
many helpers, five disabled children learn to
perform ballets. (6–9)

How to Paint
the Portrait of a Bird
by Jacques Prévert,
trans. and ill. by Mordicai Gerstein
(Roaring Brook, $16.95) 978-1-59643-215-4
Fanciful instructions to a child—in the form
of a famous poem—yield a magical painting
of a bird. (7–10)

Jazz on a Saturday Night
written and ill. by Leo & Diane Dillon
(Blue Sky, $16.99) 978-0-590-47893-9
Graphic paintings and an explanatory CD
enhance the rhyming, explosive text, which
will encourage readers to listen to more great
jazz. (7–10)

★Let it Shine:
three favorite spirituals
ill. by Ashley Bryan
(Atheneum, $16.99) 978-0-689-84732-5
"Let it Shine," "When the Saints Go
Marching In," "He's Got the Whole World in
His Hands"—all celebrated in brilliant col-
lages. (7–12)

Lift Every Voice and Sing
ill. by Bryan Collier,
written by James Weldon Johnson
(Amistad, $16.99) 978-0-06-054147-7
Inspired by the challenge of Hurricane
Katrina, Collier's striking collages offer a fresh
interpretation of the "Negro National
Anthem." Music included. (5–8)

Old Penn Station
written and ill. by William Low
(Henry Holt, $16.95) 978-0-8050-7925-8
Clear text and subtly colored, highly textured
illustrations create a rich picture of a lost
architectural treasure. (8–10)

★On My Block:
Stories And Paintings
By Fifteen Artists
edited by Dana Goldberg
(Children's Book Press, $16.95)
978-0-89239-220-9
Brief autobiographies of diverse artists illustrate their origins in their individual styles.
(8–12)

Who Put the B in the Ballyhoo?:
The Most Amazing, Bizarre, and
Celebrated Circus Performers
written and ill. by Carlyn Beccia
(HMC, $16) 978-0-618-71718-7
Dynamic poster-art illustrations follow the
many characters and features of the circus
from A to Z. (6–8)

Winter in White:
A Mini Pop-Up Treat
written and ill. by Robert Sabuda,
paper engineering by Robert Sabuda
(Little Simon, $12.99) 978-0-689-85365-4
Dance in the snow, ride a sled and celebrate
the joy of winter with this small, clever and
entertaining example of pop-up art.

BIOGRAPHY

★Anne Frank:
The Young Writer
Who Told The World Her Story
by Ann Kramer
(National Geographic, $17.95)
978-1-4263-0004-2
Details of the happy, accomplished childhood
and the tragic ending of the renowned teenag-
er. Informative photographs. (12–14)

Delicious:
The Life & Art
of Wayne Thiebaud
by Susan Goldman Rubin
(Chronicle, $15.95) 978-0-8118-5168-8
Reproductions and text on colorful pages
make this warm life history accessible and
appealing. (7–11)

Down The Colorado:
John Wesley Powell,
The One-Armed Explorer
written and ill. by Deborah Kogan Ray
(FSG, $17) 978-0-374-31838-3
A Civil War hero overcomes disability to navigate a dangerous river through the Grand
Canyon and spends the rest of his life defend-
ing that natural environment. (8–12)

E. E. Cummings:
a poet's life
by Catherine Reef
(Clarion, $21) '06 978-0-618-56849-9
An exceptional account of a very original
twentieth-century literary figure is enhanced
by well-chosen photographs. End notes, glossary and bibliography. (11–14)

George Washington Carver:
An Innovative Life
by Elizabeth MacLeod
(Kids Can, $14.95) 978-1-55337-906-5
The early struggle and later accomplishments
of a gifted, intelligent man are portrayed
along with archival photographs. (8–12)

Harriet Tubman:
Hero of the
Underground Railroad
by Lori Mortensen, ill. by Frances Moore
(Picture Window, $17.95) 978-1-4048-3103-2
This heroic African-American woman escaped
slavery and then risked her life to free others.
Includes a timeline, glossary and list of recom-
mended books. (6–9)

Helen Keller:
Her Life in Pictures
by George Sullivan
(Scholastic, $17.99) 978-0-439-91815-2
The life and work of this remarkable woman
and her teachers are depicted in a well
researched text and archival photographs.
(8–12)

★Henry David Thoreau
by Milton Meltzer
(Twenty-First Century Books, $31.93)
978-0-8225-5893-9
The life of the naturalist, teacher, abolitionist,
surveyor, and writer is presented along with a
glossary, notes and further reading. (12–14)

Louis Sockalexis:
Native American
Baseball Pioneer
by Bill Wise, ill. by Bill Farnsworth
(Lee & Low, $16.95) 978-1-58430-269-8
In the late 1800s, the first Native American on
a major league baseball team answers racial
taunting with the power of his bat. Realistic
oil paintings. (7–10)

The Many Rides of Paul Revere
by James Cross Giblin
(Scholastic, $17.99) 978-0-439-57290-3
The many contributions and dedication of the
multi-faceted Boston resident help explain the
success of the American Revolution. Archival
photographs. (11–14)

Morris and Buddy:
The Story of the
First Seeing Eye Dog
by Becky Hall, ill. by Doris Ettlinger
(Albert Whitman, $15.95) 978-0-8075-5284-1
The story of how Morris Frank started the
first American seeing eye dog school. (7–10)

Nancy Pelosi:
First Woman Speaker
of the House
by Lisa Tucker McElroy
(Lerner, $23.93) 978-0-8225-8685-2
And account of her childhood as a daughter
of a Baltimore politician is followed by her
role as a Congressional leader. Includes photographs and direct quotations. (9–14)

Our Country's First Ladies
by Ann Bausum
(National Geographic, $19.95)
978-1-4263-0006-6
This is a collection of interesting facts about
the women who occupied the White House.
Archival photographs. (9–12)

★Pass It Down:
Five Picture-Book Families
Make Their Mark
edited by Leonard S. Marcus
(Walker, $19.95) 978-0-8027-9600-4
Vivid interviews, photographs and art samples
describe five multigenerational creative picture book families. (9–13)

Patience Wright:
America's First Sculptor And
Revolutionary Spy
by Pegi Deitz Shea, ill. by Bethanne Andersen
(Henry Holt, $17.95) 978-0-8050-6770-5
In 1770s London, Wright learns secrets about
government policies and sends messages back
to America in her wax sculptures. Handsome
gouache and pastel illustrations. (8–11)

Raymond Briggs 2005

Win:
The Story Of Althea Gibson
by Karen Deans, ill. by Elbrite Brown
(Holiday House, $16.95) 978-0-8234-1926-5
Grit and determination pay off in this inspiring story of the African-American tennis
champion. Mixed-media illustrations. (6–8)

The Real Benedict Arnold
by Jim Murphy
(Clarion, $20) 978-0-395-77609-4
A seldom presented view of the famous
American traitor which attempts to explain, if
not excuse, his defection during the American
Revolution. (12–15)

The Remarkable Rough-Riding
Life Of Theodore Roosevelt And
The Rise Of Empire America
written and ill. by Cheryl Harness
(National Geographic, $16.95)
978-1-4263-0008-0
From timid boyhood to Harvard, buffalo
hunting, politics and war--the life of a famed
American is explained. Chronology and bibliography included. (8–12)

Ricardo's Race
by Diane Gonzales Bertrand,
ill. by Anthony Accardo
(Piñata, $15.95) 978-1-55885-481-9
Ricardo Romo's dedication to his family and
his athletic and educational accomplishments
is inspiring. Bilingual. (8–11)

Satchel Paige:
Don't Look Back
by David A. Adler, ill. by Terry Widener
(Harcourt, $16) 978-0-15-205585-1
The star pitcher of the Negro League was
finally admitted into the majors at the age of
forty-five. Expressive acrylics. (6–9)

Sawdust And Spangles:
The Amazing Life Of W. C. Coup
by Ralph Covert, and G. Riley Mills,
ill. by Giselle Potter
(Abrams, $16.95) 978-0-8109-9351-8
The circus pioneer's accomplishments and
passion for the 1800s big top includes the
development of the circus train and the N.Y.
Aquarium. (7–10)

The Snow Baby: The Arctic Childhood of Admiral Robert E. Peary's Daring Daughter

by Katherine Kirkpatrick
(Holiday House, $16.95) 978-0-8234-1973-9
Marie Ahnighito spends parts of her childhood in the Arctic. Includes bibliography, source notes and interesting photographs. (8–12)

★Sweet Land of Liberty

by Deborah Hopkinson,
ill. by Leonard Jenkins
(Peachtree, $16.95) 978-1-56145-395-5
A new wrinkle in Marian Anderson's story focuses on Oscar Chapman, Assistant Secretary of the Interior, who arranged the Lincoln Memorial concert. (8–11)

Up Close: Johnny Cash: Music Legend

by Anne E. Neimark
(Viking, $15.99) 978-0-670-06215-7
The details of the country music icon's difficult but colorful life will both inspire and caution readers. (9–12)

★Walker Evans: Photographer of America

by Thomas Nau
(Roaring Brook, $19.95) 978-1-59643-225-3
The photographer of "life as he saw it" is portrayed in words and photographs. Citations and bibliography. (9–12)

We Are One: The Story of Bayard Rustin

by Larry Dane Brimner
(Boyds Mills, $17.95) 978-1-59078-498-3
Clear text and archival photographs fully explain the life of this fighter who fought against injustice through nonviolent action. (9–13)

ECOLOGY

Coral Reefs

written and ill. by Gail Gibbons
(Holiday House, $16.95) 978-0-8234-2080-3
Samples of life from coral reefs around the world illustrate a beautiful and vital endangered environment. Watercolors. (5–8)

★One Well: The Story of Water on Earth

by Rochelle Strauss, ill. by Rosemary Woods
(Kids Can, $17.95) 978-1-55337-954-6
Delicate illustrations accompany facts and an appeal to care about our connected world. (7–10)

★Tracking Trash: Flotsam, Jetsam, and the Science of Ocean Motion

by Loree Griffin Burns
(HMC, $18) 978-0-618-58131-3
Floating sneakers, turkeys, fishnets and laundry baskets all help scientists learn about currents and how we can protect our oceans. (8–12)

HEALTH

The Boy's Body Book

by Kelli Dunham, ill. by Steve Bjorkman
(Cider Mill, $9.95) 978-1-933662-74-9
From smelly feet to changing voices, a simple, honest collection of puberty issues is presented. (9–14)

Inside Out: Portrait Of An Eating Disorder

written and ill. by Nadia Shivack
(Atheneum, $17.99) 978-0-689-85216-9
The author's struggle with bulimia is graphically described. (12–15)

Tic Talk: Living with Tourette Syndrome

by Dylan Peters, ill. by Zachary Wendland
(Little Five Star, $14.95) 978-1-58985-051-4
A nine-year-old, a baseball player and a teacher tell about their experiences and give strategies for handling the neurological disease that involves uncontrollable body movements. Additional resources. (9–12)

HISTORY

1607: A New Look At Jamestown

by Karen E. Lange, photos by Ira Block
(National Geographic, $17.95) 1-4263-0012-3
Recent archeological discoveries present new insights into the history, problems and positive attributes of America's oldest settlement. (9–12)

⬛★America Dreaming: How Youth Changed America in the '60s

by Laban Carrick Hill
(Little, $19.99) 978-0-316-00904-1
Filled with documentary photos, strong graphics, and primary sources, this is a kaleidoscopic look at history, music, art, culture and politics in a turbulent time. (12–14)

Joshua Chamberlain and the American Civil War

by Robert F. Kennedy, Jr.,
ill. by Nikita Andreev
(Hyperion, $16.99) 978-1-4231-0771-2
Learn about this extremely brave and skillful leader and his inspiring devotion to his men and the Union cause. (10–13)

Hidden on the Mountain: Stories of Children Sheltered from the Nazis in Le Chambon

by Deborah Durland DeSaix
and Karen Gray Ruelle
(Holiday House, $24.95) 978-0-8234-1928-9
During World War II, the people in a small French farming community sheltered children and kept them safe from the Nazis. Told from interviews. Archival photographs, bibliography and maps. (10–14)

Lightship

written and ill. by Brian Floca
(Atheneum, $16.99) 978-1-4169-2436-4
Witty, vibrant paintings tell how a lightship crew helped ships to navigate safely. (4–7)

Puerto Rico

by Ruth Bjorklund
(Cavendish, $20.95) 978-0-7614-2218-1
History, flora and fauna, government and the economy are all accompanied by color photographs. (9–11)

River Roads West: America's First Highways

by Peter Roop and Connie Roop
(Calkins Creek, $19.95) 978-1-59078-430-3
America's desire to find a northwest passage to the Pacific leads explorers through the extraordinary major rivers of our nation. (10–13)

The Secret of Priest's Grotto: A Holocaust Survival Story

by Peter Lane Taylor, with Christos Nicola
(Kar-Ben, $18.95) 1-58013-260-2
Buttons, shoes and a house key are discovered in a Ukranian cave where Jewish families hid from the Nazis. (10–14)

The Ultimate Weapon: The Race To Develop The Atomic Bomb

by Edward T. Sullivan
(Holiday House, $24.95) 978-0-8234-1855-8
Many scientific, political and social developments contributed to the creation of the atomic bomb, as explained in this thorough account. (12–14)

⬛ The Wall: Growing Up Behind The Iron Curtain

written and ill. by Peter Sís
(FSG, $18) 978-0-374-34701-7
A compelling pictorial memoir of the author's childhood and adolescence in Czechoslovakia during the Cold War and the Russian occupation. (12–14)

★War Women and the News: How Female Journalists Won the Battle to Cover World War II

by Catherine Gourley
(Atheneum, $21.99) 978-0-689-87752-0
The rise of female journalists and their work reporting on World War II. (12–14)

★Who Was First?: Discovering the Americas

by Russell Freedman
(Clarion, $19) 978-0-618-66391-0
The theories about who came to America, and when and where they landed, are presented along with a discussion of the earliest Native Americans. Bibliography and archival photographs. (10–14)

Raymond Briggs 2005

Special Interests

Angela and the Baby Jesus
by Frank McCourt, ill. by Raúl Colón
(S&S, $17.99) 978-1-4169-3789-0
The author's mother's tale follows Angela as
she rescues Baby Jesus from the local crèche
in her Irish church. Soft watercolor and colored pencil illustrations. (5–7)

The Best Eid Ever
by Asma Mobin-Uddin, ill. by Laura Jacobsen
(Boyds Mills, $16.95) 978-1-59078-431-0
A young Pakistani girl helps two recent
refugees from a war-torn country during the
Muslim holiday Eid. Colorful pastel illustrations. (6–8)

Celebrate Easter With Colored Eggs, Flowers, and Prayer
by Deborah Heiligman
(National Geographic, $15.95)
978-1-4263-0020-2
A compilation of facts, recipes, bibliographies
and photographs. (7–10)

Celebrate Hanukkah with Light, Latkes, and Dreidels
by Deborah Heiligman
(National Geographic, $15.95) '06
0-7922-5924-6
Learn why and how holidays are celebrated
around the world. (8–12)

Celebrate Passover With Matzah, Maror, And Memories
by Deborah Heiligman
(National Geographic, $15.95)
978-1-4263-0018-9
See Celebrate Easter (7–10)

Do Rabbits Have Christmas?
poems by Aileen Fisher,
ill. by Sarah Fox-Davies
(Henry Holt, $16.95) 978-0-8050-7491-8
A delightful collection of poems that celebrates the beauty of winter and the wonder of
Christmas. Warm, delicate watercolors. (5–8)

Great Joy
by Kate DiCamillo, ill. by Bagram Ibatoulline
(Candlewick, $16.99) 978-0-7636-2920-5
As Frances prepares for the Christmas pag-
eant, she worries about the organ grinder and
monkey on the corner. Poignant acrylic and
gouache illustrations. (5–8)

Letter On The Wind: A Chanukah Tale
by Sarah Marwil Lamtein,
ill. by Neil Waldman
(Boyds Mills, $16.95) 978-1-932425–74-1
Hayim has faith that God will provide the oil
needed to celebrate the Festival of Lights.
Based on a Tunisian tale. Illustrated with magical watercolors. (6–10)

Little Rabbit's Christmas
written and ill. by Harry Horse
(Peachtree, $15.95) 978-1-56145-419-8
Little Rabbit's favorite Christmas gift, a sled,
brings him some unexpected presents. Pen-
and-ink and watercolor illustrations. (5–7)

N Is for Navidad
by Susan Middleton Elya, and Merry Banks,
ill. by Joe Cepeda
(Chronicle, $14.95) 978-0-8118-5205-0
Lively illustrations and text show how to celebrate a Latino Christmas from A to Z. (5–7)

MATH

★It's Probably Penny
written and ill. by Loreen Leedy
(Henry Holt, $16.95) 978-0-8050-7389-2
The concept of probability is explained, along
with useful information about making predic-
tions. (8–14)

A Second Is A Hiccup: A Child's Book Of Time
by Hazel Hutchins,
ill. by Kady MacDonald Denton
(Arthur A. Levine, $16.99) 978-0-439-83106-2
Time explained in terms of children's familiar
activities. Watercolor and ink illustrations.
(4–7)

Hiromi's Hands
by Lynne Barasch
(Lee & Low, $17.95) 1-58430-275-9
The father of a Japanese-American girl trains her to be a sushi chef, breaking with tradition. Ink and watercolor illustrations. (5–8)

The House of a Million Pets
by Ann Hodgman, ill. by Eugene Yelchin
(Henry Holt, $16.95) 978-0-8050-7974-6
The author shares the pleasures and hard work of caring for a range of animals. (9–12)

PARENTS AND CHILDREN

Could You? Would You?: A Book to Tickle your Imagination
written and ill. by Trudy White
(Kane/Miller, $12.95) 978-1-933605-45-6
Posed questions provoke laughter, thought, drawings and other ways of explaining the world. Simple ink and wash drawings. (6–8)

Mr. Gauguin's Heart
by Marie-Danielle Croteau, ill. by Isabelle Arsenault, trans. by Susan Ouriou
(Tundra, $18.95) 978-0-88776-824-8
Mourning his father, little Paul Gauguin is able to transform his grief into a picture, the first of many. (6–9)

Please Is A Good Word To Say
by Barbara Joosse, ill. by Jennifer Plecas
(Philomel, $12.99) 978-0-399-24217-5
A humorous approach teaches children how to use polite words and expressions. Cartoon-like illustrations. (4–6)

★The Purple Balloon
written and ill. by Chris Raschka
(S & W, $16.99) 978-0-375-84146-0
The community of caregivers surrounding a dying child is compassionately presented for the very young. Reassuring illustrations. (5–8)

★Sleepy Little Yoga
by Rebecca Whitford, ill. by Martina Selway
(Henry Holt, $9.95) 978-0-8050-8193-0
Toddlers and animals are matched in gentle yoga positions. Simple, colorful illustrations. (1–4)

Sophie's Big Bed
written and ill. by Tina Burke
(Kane/Miller, $4.99) 978-1-933605-48-7
Sophie and her doll and animal friends like her crib and are wary of her new bigger bed. (2–4)

POETRY

★Animal Poems
by Valerie Worth, ill. by Steve Jenkins
(FSG, $17) 978-0-374-38057-1
Rich, interesting language and finely detailed, cut-paper collages bring a diverse menagerie to life. (8–14)

★Behind the Museum Door: Poems to Celebrate the Wonders of Museums
selected by Lee Bennett Hopkins, ill. by Stacey Dressen-McQueen
(Abrams, $16.95) 978-0-8109–1204-5
Renowned poets highlight such museum treasures as mummies and medieval relics, fine art and fossils. Colorful acrylic, pastel and colored pencil illustrations. (7–10)

★Birmingham, 1963
by Carole Boston Weatherford
(Wordsong, $17.95) 978-1-59078-440-2
A fictional ten-year-old witness describes her feelings at the scene of the devastating Alabama bombing. Powerful words and archival photographs. (9–12)

★Blue Lipstick: Concrete Poems
by John Grandits
(Clarion, $15) 978-0-618-56860-4
Wry, varied, and humorous concrete poems reveal a high school student's musings on her life. (9–14)

Bronzeville Boys and Girls
by Gwendolyn Brooks, ill. by Faith Ringgold
(HarperCollins, $16.99) 978-0-06-029505–9
A lively re-illustrated edition of a collection celebrating the joys of childhood, originally published in 1956. (6–9)

Special Interests

Collected Poems for Children
by Ted Hughes, ill. by Raymond Briggs
(FSG, $18) 978-0-374-31429-3
250 demanding but engaging and often funny poems written throughout the Poet Laureate's lifetime. Sketchy black and white drawings. (8–12)

★Comets, Stars, the Moon, and Mars: Space Poems and Paintings
written and ill. by Douglas Florian
(Harcourt, $16) 978-0-15-205372-7
Descriptions of what can be seen in outer space. Bright gouache and collage illustrations. (6–9)

Dog Poems
by Dave Crawley, ill. by Tamara Petrosino
(Wordsong, $16.95) 978-1-59078-454-9
The canine world is humorously conveyed with these varied poems and cartoon-like illustrations. (4–7)

Dogku
by Andrew Clements, ill. by Tim Bowers
(S&S, $16.99) 978-0-689-85823-9
Will this adorable dog find a home? The answer is in these charming haiku poems. Humorous illustrations. (5–8)

★Good Sports: Rhymes about Running, Jumping, Throwing and More
by Jack Prelutsky, ill. by Chris Raschka
(Knopf, $16.99) 978-0-375–83700-5
Catchy, appealing rhythms and rhymes are accompanied by watercolors brimming with energy and motion. (6–9)

★Here's A Little Poem: A Very First Book Of Poetry
collected by Jane Yolen and
Andrew Fusek Peters, ill. by Polly Dunbar
(Candlewick, $21.99) 978-0-7636-3141-3
High-quality, exuberant poems and multimedia illustrations introduce young children to this genre. (3–5)

Hey, You!: Poems to Skyscrapers, Mosquitoes, and Other Fun Things
selected by Paul B. Janeczko,
ill. by Robert Rayevsky
(HarperCollins, $15.99) 978-0-06-052347-3
Thirty familiar objects are viewed with a poet's fresh eyes. Witty paintings. (8–11)

★Holiday Stew: A kid's portion of holiday and seasonal poems
written and ill. by Jenny Whitehead
(Henry Holt, $17.95) 978-0-8050-7715-5
From Thanksgiving to Christmas, Passover and Ramadan, poems are enhanced with humorous illustrations. (5–9)

★Jabberwocky: The Classic Poem from Lewis Carroll's Through the Looking-Glass, and What Alice Found There
reimagined and ill. by Christopher Myers
(Jump At The Sun, $15.99)
978-14-142310372-1
Christopher Myers discovers the hip-hop beat in Lewis Carroll's classic nonsense poem, reimagining it in the urban world of jump rope and basketball. (9–12)

Maya Angelou: Poetry for Young People
edited by Edwin Graves Wilson,
ill. by Jerome Lagarrigue
(Sterling, $14.95) 978-1-4027-2023-9
Selected poems dealing with her African-American heritage by one of the most celebrated American writers. (11–14)

Raymond Briggs 2005

★Miss Crandall's School for Young Ladies & Little Misses of Color

poems by Elizabeth Alexander and Marilyn Nelson, ill. by Floyd Cooper (Wordsong, $17.95) 978-1-59078-456-3
The harsh story of the first school for African-American girls in 1830s Connecticut is told in poems from different viewpoints. (12–14) M

★Mother Goose: Numbers on the Loose

compiled and ill. by Leo & Diane Dillon (Harcourt, $17) 978-0-15-205676-6
This collection of numeric nursery rhymes is illustrated with glowing art. (2–5)

★My Grandma Likes to Say

by Denise Brennan-Nelson, ill. by Jane Monroe Donovan (Sleeping Bear, $16.95) 978-1-58536-284-4
The poetry of Grandma's sayings reflects a child's literal interpretation. Origins and meanings are provided. Humorous illustrations. (8–12)

Nature's Paintbox: A Seasonal Gallery Of Art And Verse

by Patricia Thomas, ill. by Craig Orback (Millbrook, $16.95) 978-0-8225-6807-0
Each season is rendered in rich verse and illustrated in various media. (7–10)

★Oh, Theodore!: Guinea Pig Poems

by Susan Katz, ill. by Stacey Schuett (Clarion, $16) 978-0-618-70222-0
Simple poetic text rhythmically explores a boy's rewards of caring for a pet. Acrylic paint and gouache illustrations. (5–8)

The Owl and the Pussycat

by Edward Lear, ill. by Stéphane Jorisch (Kids Can, $9.95) 978-1-55453-232-2
The much-loved Lear poem is illustrated in a contemporary style. (9–14)

A Sea-Wishing Day

by Robert Heidbreder, ill. by Kady MacDonald Denton (Kids Can, $15.95) 978-1-55337-707-8
A child's longing for adventure leads him and his dog on a poetic fantasy voyage to the sea—and back. Expressive gouache illustrations. (3–6)

The Snack Smasher and Other Reasons Why It's Not My Fault

by Andrea Perry, ill. by Alan Snow (Atheneum, $16.99) 978-0-689-85469-9
Mischievous creatures wreak havoc in children's lives. Amusing rhymes and zany colorful pen and ink illustrations. (5–8)

Tap Dancing on the Roof: Sijo (Poems)

by Linda Sue Park, pictures by Istvan Banyai (Clarion, $16) 978-0-618-23483-7
Everyday occurrences are described in traditional Korean verse. Imaginative digital illustrations. (7–10)

★This Is Just to Say: Poems of Apology and Forgiveness

by Joyce Sidman, ill. by Pamela Zagarenski (HMC, $16) 978-0-618-61680-0
Poems of children's apologies are paired with responses of forgiveness. Mixed-media journal-page illustrations. (6–12)

Raymond Briggs 2005

Toad By The Road: A Year In The Life Of These Amazing Amphibians

by Joanne Ryder, ill. by Maggie Kneen
(Henry Holt, $16.95) 0-8050-7354-X
Learn about these amphibians as simple verse and soft detailed watercolors follow them through the seasons. (5–8)

★Today and Today

by Kobayashi Issa, ill. by G. Brian Karas
(Scholastic, $16.99) 978-0-439-59078-5
Japanese haiku celebrate the everyday joys and sorrows of one family's life. Pencil and paint on rice paper illustrations. (7–12)

Trailblazers: Poems of Exploration

by Bobbi Katz, ill. by Carin Berger
(Greenwillow, $18.99) 978-0-688-16533-8
The struggles, excitement and adventures of explorers of all ages, past and present. Biographies appended. (9–14)

Twist: Yoga Poems

by Janet S. Wong, ill. by Julie Paschkis
(McElderry, $17.99) 978-0-689-87394-2
Clear, evocative verses and miniature Indian-inspired illustrations bring traditional sketches and poses to life.

We

by Alice Schertle, ill. by Kenneth Addison
(Lee & Low, $16.95) 978-1-58430-060-1
Human development is traced from its beginnings millions of years ago in Africa to modern times. Fascinating mixed-media collages. (12–14)

When Gorilla Goes Walking

by Nikki Grimes, ill. by Shane Evans
(Orchard, $16.99) 978-0-439-31770-2
Cecilia, the girl, describes Cecilia, the cat, in simple rhymes with humorous illustrations. (4–6)

★Where I Live

by Eileen Spinelli, ill. by Matt Phelan
(Dial, $16.99) 978-0-8037-3122-6
Diana's life is disrupted when her father loses his job and the family must move. Endearing black-and-white illustrations. (6–9)

Young Cornrows Callin out the Moon

by Ruth Forman, ill. by Cbabi Bayoc
(Children's Book Press, $16.95)
978-0-89239-218-6
Visit summer on the streets of South Philly—kids, double dutch and the ice cream truck. Bold, vibrant illustrations. (6–8)

Yum! ¡MmMm! ¡Que Rico!: Americas' Sproutings

Haiku by Pat Mora, pictures by Rafael López
(Lee & Low, $16.95) 978-1-58430-271-1
Lush, vibrant illustrations accompany a collection of haiku and side-bar notes celebrating the indigenous foods of the Americas. (8–10)

REFERENCE

Golden Legacy: How Golden Books Won Children's Hearts, Changed Publishing Forever, and Became an American Icon Along the Way

by Leonard S. Marcus,
foreword by Eric Carle
(Golden Books, $40) 978-0-375-82996-3
This thorough, artfully designed account of the immensely popular children's book publisher is chock-full of rich nuggets of history. (Adult)

Greedy Apostrophe: A Cautionary Tale

by Jan Carr, ill. by Ethan Long
(Holiday House, $16.95) 978-0-8234-2006-3
Possessives? Contractions? Just when are different punctuation marks needed? (9–11)

Our 50 United States and Other U.S. Lands

by Renée Skelton, and Jaime Joyce
(HarperCollins, $17.99) 978-0-06-081557-8
Facts about the states and territories are supported by maps, archival illustrations and photographs. (10–12)

Woe Is I Jr.: The Younger Grammarphobe's Guide to Better English

by Patricia T. O'Conner
(Putnam, $16.99) 978-0-399-24331-8
Word choices and punctuation of English are explained with humor and imagination. (10–14)

★Writing Magic: Creating Stories That Fly

by Gail Carson Levine
(HarperCollins, $16.99) '06 978-0-06-051961-2
The many aspects of the writing process are presented with clarity and humor. Useful tips and exercises. (10–12)

RELIGION

My Father's House

by Kathi Appelt, ill. by Raúl Colón
(Viking, $16.99) 978-0-670-03669-1
Vibrant, joyous illustrations accompany a poetic prayer of praise to the Creator. (4–7)

Shouting!

by Joyce Carol Thomas, ill. by Annie Lee
(Jump At The Sun, $16.99)
978-0-7868-0664-8
A mother and daughter participate in a celebration of life, faith and hope in services at an African-American church. Colorful, impressionistic illustrations. (6–10)

SCIENCE

ABC Safari

written and ill. by Karen Lee
(Sylvan Dell, $15.95) 978-0-9777423-0-1
Clever poems introduce creatures in a wide variety of habitats. Accurate illustrations with reproducible cards. (5–8)

Ape

by Martin Jenkins, ill. by Vicky White
(Candlewick, $16.99) 978-0-7636-3471-1
The five great apes are captured in strong pencil and oil illustrations. Brief informative text. (5–7)

★Apples

by Jacqueline Farmer,
ill. by Phyllis Limbacher Tildes
(Charlesbridge, $16.95) 978-1-57091-694-6
The farming, varieties and history of the most popular fruit in the United States. Colorful watercolor and pencil illustrations. (5–8)

The Bald Eagle

by Norman Pearl, ill. by Matthew Skeens
(Picture Window, P$8.95) 978-1-4048-2642-7
The history and biology of America's national emblem in simple text and engaging cartoon-style illustrations. (5–8)

Cave Detectives: Unraveling The Mystery Of An Ice Age Cave

by David L. Harrison, ill. by Ashley Mims, photos by Edward Biamonte
(Chronicle, $15.95) 978-0-8118-5006-3
A paleontologist team unravels the mysteries of prehistoric times at the Riverbluff Cave in Missouri. (9–12)

Circulating Life: Blood Transfusion from Ancient Superstition to Modern Medicine

by Cherie Winner
(Twenty-First Century Books, $29.27)
978-0-8225-6606–9
Scientists and their practices, from blood-letting to AIDS, provide a fascinating history. Includes detailed physiology of the blood, glossary, index and helpful illustrations and photos. (12–14)

Deserts

by Cathryn Sill, ill. by John Sill
(Peachtree, $16.95) 978-1-56145-390-0
Flora and fauna grow in these dry places. Clear, watercolor illustrations. (4–7)

The Down-to-Earth Guide to Global Warming

by Laurie David, and Cambria Gordon
(Orchard, $15.99) 978-0-439-02494-5
The text, photographs, maps and charts clearly explain the causes and effects of global warming and ways in which we work together to stop it. (11–14)

★EMI and the Rhino Scientist

by Mary Kay Carson, photos by Tom Uhlman
(HMC, $18) 978-0-618-64639-5
Conservationists discover how to save the rare and endangered Sumatran rhinoceros. (8–12)

A Giraffe Grows Up

by Amanda Doering Tourville,
ill. by Michael Denman & William J. Huiett
(Picture Window, $25.26) 978-1-4048-3158-2
A giraffe's journey from birth through adulthood. Simple facts and realistic acrylic illustrations. (4–7)

Guess What Is Growing Inside This Egg

written and ill. by Mia Posada
(Millbrook, $15.95) 978-0-8225-6192-7
Easy rhymes create a guessing game about animals and their babies. Illuminated by watercolor collages. (4–7)

Hello, Bumblebee Bat

by Darrin Lunde, ill. by Patricia J. Wynne
(Charlesbridge, $15.95) 978-1-57091-374–7
Clear language and detailed watercolor with colored pencil illustrations describe the world's smallest bat. (4–6)

A Horse in the House and Other Strange but True Animal Stories

by Gail Ablow, ill. by Kathy Osborn
(Candlewick, $17.99) 978-0-7636-2838-3
A collection based on newspaper stories about humans, animals and the wacky things they do together. Colorful and surreal gouache paintings.

★An Inconvenient Truth: The Crisis Of Global Warming

by Al Gore
(Viking, $23) 978-0-670-06271-3
Al Gore's famed bestseller is adapted for a younger audience with simple text and clear photographs and diagrams. (10–14)

It's a Butterfly's Life

written and ill. by Irene Kelly
(Holiday House, $16.95) 978-0-8234-1860-2
The process of metamorphosis is told with interesting details and colorful, accurate drawings. (8–10)

The Jumbo Book of Space

by Cynthia Pratt Nicolson and Paulette Bourgeois, ill. by Bill Slavin
(Kids Can, $17.95) 1-55453-020-5
Interesting facts about space are presented in a question and answer format. (8–10)

Knut: How One Little Polar Bear Captivated the World

told by Juliana Hatkoff, Isabella Hatkoff, Craig Hatkoff and Dr. Gerald R. Uhlich
(Scholastic, $16.99) 978-0-545-04716-6
A bear keeper raises a cuddly cub, born in a German zoo. Brilliant, full-color photographs by Zoo Berlin. (5–7)

★Life-Size Reptiles

by Hannah Wilson
(Sterling, $9.95) 978-1-4027-4542-3
A plethora of well-organized information is accompanied by colorful, detailed illustrations, many of which are life-size. (4–10)

Lungs: Your Respiratory System

by Seymour Simon
(Smithsonian Institution, $16.99)
978-0-06-054654-0
Find out how the lungs work. Useful, clear photographs, diagrams and illustrations. (9–12)

Meet The Meerkat

by Darrin Lunde, ill. by Patricia J. Wynne
(Charlesbridge, $15.95) 978-1-58089-110-3
Basic information about this less well-known animal for the youngest audience. Expressive watercolor illustrations. (5–7)

My, Oh My—a Butterfly!: All About Butterflies

by Tish Rabe, ill. by Aristides Ruiz and Joe Mathieu
(Random, $8.99) 978-0-375–82882-9
The life cycle written in Dr. Seuss's style. Glossary and suggestions for further reading. (4–7)

Ocean Seasons

by Ron Hirschi, ill. by Kirsten Carlson
(Sylvan Dell, $15.95) 978-0-9777423-2-5
Vivid and realistic illustrations beautifully capture the life cycle of creatures in the Pacific Ocean. (3–6)

Owen & Mzee:
The Language Of Friendship
by Isabella Hatkoff, Craig Hatkoff and
Paula Kahumbu, photos by Peter Greste
(Scholastic, $16.99) 978-0-439-89959-8
The unusual friendship between the old tor-
toise and the young hippo continues as a system of communication develops between
them. (7–10)

Penguins
by Seymour Simon, photos
(HarperCollins/Smithsonian, $17.89)
978--06-028396-4
The natural life of this Antarctic bird is
described and accompanied by excellent photographs. (8–11)

A Seed Is Sleepy
by Dianna Hutts Aston, ill. by Sylvia Long
(Chronicle, $16.95) 978-0-8118-5520-4
A guide to seed and plant facts presented
through simple but detailed text and large ink
and watercolor illustrations. (5–7)

Spiders
by Nic Bishop
(Scholastic, $16.99) 978-0-439-87756-5
Extraordinary close-up photographs and a
wealth of information enhance this interesting
book. (5–8)

Superbugs Strike Back:
When Antibiotics Fail
by Connie Goldsmith
(Twenty-First Century Books, $30.60)
978-0-8225-6607-6
This study about resistant strains of infection-
causing bacteria includes the latest scientific
research, a glossary and a website. (12–14)

Tiger's Story
by Harriet Blackford, ill. by Manya Stojic
(Boxer Books, $12.95) 978-1-905417-39-1
Impressionistic illustrations chronicle the animal's life from cub to independence in the
forests of India. (4–6)

★Tough, Toothy Baby Sharks
by Sandra Markle
(Walker, $16.95) 978-0-8027-9593-9
The life story of these unusual fish is accompanied by revealing underwater photographs.
(9–12)

Turtle Summer:
A Journal For My Daughter
by Mary Alice Monroe, photos by
Barbara J. Bergwerf, ill. by Lisa Downey
(Sylvan Dell, $15.95) 978-0-9777423-5-6
A summer spent helping to insure the survival
of endangered loggerhead turtles is recorded
in text, photographs and drawings. Includes
facts and activities. (7–10)

★Twilight Hunt:
A Seek-and-Find Book
written and ill. by Narelle Oliver
(Star Bright, $16.95) '07 978-1-59572-107-5
Linocut illustrations demonstrate the impor-
tance of animal camouflage for survival in
nature as a screech owl searches for supper.
(5–8)

Vulture View
by April Pulley Sayre, ill. by Steve Jenkins
(Henry Holt, $16.95) 978-0-8050-7557-1
Rhyming text and cut paper collages convey a
great deal of information about these birds.
(6–8)

Wetlands Soggy Habitat
by Laura Purdie Salas, ill. by Jeff Yesh
(Picture Window, $25.26) 978-1-4048-3100-1
This journey takes us into the delicate and
unique environment where some land meets
the sea. (6–9)

★The Whale Scientists:
Solving the Mystery of
Whale Strandings
by Fran Hodgkins, photos
(HMC, $18) 978-0-618-55673-1
A well-documented and fascinating account of
how scientists are striving to discover why
whales run aground. (8–12)

- ## STATES OF MATTER

What Is a Gas?

What Is a Liquid?

What Is a Solid?
by Jennifer Boothroyd
(Lerner, $17.27) NE 978-0-8225-6837-7,978-0-8225-6838-1, 978-0-8225-6836-5
The different properties of matter are introduced with vibrant photographs, concise descriptions and early reader sentences. (5–7)

When Is a Planet Not a Planet?: The Story of Pluto
by Elaine Scott
(Clarion, $17) 978-0-618-89832-9
Striking photographs aid us in discovering how scientists changed their thinking about the ninth planet. (8–11)

★Where In The Wild?: Camouflaged Creatures Concealed. . . and Revealed
by David M. Schwartz and Yael Schy, photos by Dwight Kuhn
(Tricycle, $15.95) 978-1-58246-207-3
Creatures, both on the move and hidden, are revealed by lifting flaps. (5–10)

- ## EXPLORING THE ELEMENTS

Who Likes The Rain?

Who Likes the Sun?
by Etta Kaner, ill. by Marie Lafrance
(Kids Can, $14.95) 978-1-55337-841-9, 978-1-55337-840-2
Everyday thoughts are revealed under flaps that provide detailed information about scientific processes. Simple acrylic illustrations. (5–7)

SPORTS

Capoeira
written and photographed by George Ancona
(Lee & Low, $18.95) 978-1-58430-268-1
Why must one have a nickname to play? Learn the answer and more about this Brazilian game, martial art and dance. Vibrant photographs. (6–8)

Jesse Owens: Fastest Man Alive
by Carole Boston Weatherford, ill. by Eric Velasquez
(Walker, $17.85) 978-0-8027-9551-9
A great athlete triumphs in the Berlin Olympics. Includes background history and bibliography. (7–10)

Surfer of the Century: The Life of Duke Kahanamoku
by Ellie Crowe, ill. by Richard Waldrep
(Lee & Low, $18.95) 978-1-58430-276-6
A Hawaiian swimmer overcomes racism and his own shyness to become an Olympic superstar. (8–12)

WORLD

New York: The Empire State
by Margery Facklam, and Peggy Thomas, ill. by Jon Messer
(Charlesbridge, $16.95) 978-1-57091-660-1
Odd and interesting facts about this great city, accompanied by detailed illustrations. (8–10)

Wonders of the World
by Philip Steele,
foreword by Françoise Rivière
(Kingfisher, $12.95) 978-0-7534-5979-9
Ancient and modern examples of very special places throughout the world are expressed through art, architecture and natural phenomena. (10–12)

Yatandou: Mali, Africa
by Gloria Whelan, paintings by Peter Sylvada
(Sleeping Bear, $17.95) 978-1-58536-211-0
Eight-year-old Yatandou works much of the day in her village in Mali, pounding millet as village women care for their families. Impressionistic illustrations. (7–10)

Special Interests

Index

Index

Index

54

Index

57

PUBLISHERS

Abrams
Aladdin
Albert Whitman
Amistad
Amulet
Arthur A. Levine
Atheneum
August House
Bay Otter
Bethany House
Bloomsbury
Blue Apple
Blue Sky
Boxer
Boyds Mills
Calkins Creek
Candlewick
Carolrhoda
Cavendish
Charlesbridge
Chicken House
Children's Book
Chronicle
Cinco Puntos
Clarion
David Fickling
Delacorte
Dial
Dutton
Enchanted Lion
Cider Mill
Eerdmans
EOS
Farrar, Straus & Giroux
Feiwel
First Second
Flashlight
Front
Golden
Graphic Universe
Greenwillow
Groundwood
Handprint
Harcourt
HarperCollins
Henry Holt
Houghton Mifflin
Holiday House
Hyperion
Jump at the Sun
Kane/Miller
Kar-Ben

Kids Can
Kingfisher
Knopf
Lark
Lee & Low
Lerner
Maple Tree
McElderry
Millbrook
Little Brown
Little Five Star
Little Simon
Mayhaven Publishing
Minedition
Miramax
National Geographic
North-South
Orchard
Peachtree
Penguin
Philomel
Picture Window
Piñata

Putnam
Random House
Rainbow Bridge
Roaring Brook
Scholastic
Schwartz & Wade
Second Story
Shenanigan
Simon & Schuster
Sleeping Bear
Star Bright
Smithsonian
Sterling Publications
Stewart, Tabori & Chang
Sylvan Dell
Tricycle
Tundra
Twenty-First Century
Viking
Walker
Wendy Lamb
Wordsong

The Children's Book Committee
Bank Street College of Education
610 West 112th Street
New York, NY 10025
212/875-4540
fax 212/875-4759
e-mail: bookcom@bankstreet.edu
website: www.bankstreet.edu/bookcom/